THE ART OF
BUILDING WORSHIP SERVICES

The Art
of Building
Worship Services

Thomas Bruce McDormand

Revised Edition

1958

BROADMAN PRESS
Nashville, Tennessee

Library of Congress catalog card number: 58–11547
Printed in the United States of America
5.MH58K.S.P.

1144898

DEDICATION

This book is affectionately dedicated to my wife, Irene, whose unselfishness, understanding, and spiritual sensitivity have made it possible for me to produce this book in the midst of a heavy schedule of regular duties.

Contents

Preface   ix

1. What Is True Worship?   1

   Worship in the Bible. Defining worship. Obstacles to
   worship. After worship—what?

2. The Parts of a Worship Service   9

   The elements in worship services. Use of suitable materials.

3. The Call to Worship   15

   From the Scriptures. From the hymnbook. From poetry.
   Hymns and poems combined. Devotional books.

4. Making the Most of Hymns   25

   Varied uses of hymns. Using interesting facts about hymns.

5. Making the Most of Scripture   46

   A call to Scripture reading. Choral readings. Using the
   newer translations. Bible mosaics. Scripture used with
   religious art. Drama with scripture reading. Using Scrip-

ture to direct silent prayer. Descriptive introduction to
Scripture lesson.

6. Prayer, the Soul of Worship   58

Calls to prayer. Great Bible prayers. Prayer hymns. Prepared prayers. The use of group or corporate prayers.
Prayers offered by individuals.

7. Stories, Biography, and Quotations   75

Stories. Biography. Quotations.

8. Ten Worship Services for Use   92

The Scriptures
The Church
Missions
Stewardship
The Christian Home
World Brotherhood
The New Year
Easter
A Christian Thanksgiving
Christmas

Preface

THIS BOOK IS OFFERED to Christian leaders with the sincere hope that it may lighten their task of preparing fruitful worship services, even while giving them greater pleasure in doing so.

Spiritually productive worship should enlighten the mind, quicken the spirit of reverence, move the heart to thankfulness and aspiration, command the will to greater discipline and obedience. These end results cannot be obtained unless worship services are rich in content, arresting and satisfying in form, and planned so as to provide for meaningful participation by every worshiper. It is with these principles in full view that this handbook has been prepared. It is offered in the sincere belief that the lives of people and the life of the Christian church will be enriched and strengthened if thoughtful use is made of the suggestions offered and the materials provided herein.

The writer gives thanks for the extensive use which has been made of former editions of this book. The present revision is extensive, with many new resource materials offered, and should make the new edition even more helpful than its forerunner.

THOMAS BRUCE McDORMAND

Toronto, Canada

1

What Is True Worship?

THIS BOOK IS DEDICATED to the proposition that worship is a primary function of the church of Jesus Christ and a basic need of God's people.

Canon Frank Russell Barry, theologian of Liverpool and Oxford chaplain to the king, wrote some years ago: "The Church, as the worshiping society and the body of Christ in the world, is to be the means of reconciliation. . . . Therefore worship 'in spirit and in truth' ought to mean a continual conversion of our thought, our standards and our aims: and it must result, in direct proportion to its vitality, richness, and sincerity, in a moral and social revolution. It follows that the justifiable criticism would be not that the Church puts worship first, but that such big areas of its life in the world are still unpenetrated by the spirit of worship." Professor George Walter Fiske, minister in the Congregational Church, educator and author, speaks even more directly and urgently when he writes, "Unless the free churches develop a more convincing, more compelling and more satisfying worship, Protestantism is doomed."

WORSHIP IN THE BIBLE

Certainly Bible-believing Christians cannot dispute the fundamental place which worship must have in the life of the people of God. From Genesis to Revelation worship occupies a central place in the life of the saints, the exhortations of the prophets, the practices of the Temple and synagogue, the life of the infant church, and, above all, in the example and teaching of our Lord and Saviour.

The Ten Commandments open with the command to exalt Jehovah above all gods.

The psalmist unceasingly summons his people to the attitude and act of worship. "O come," says he, "let us worship and bow down: let us kneel before the Lord our maker" (95:6). And again, "Know ye that the Lord he is God: it is he that hath made us, and not we ourselves. . . . Enter into his gates with thanksgiving, and into his courts with praise" (100:3–4). Once more he writes, "The fear of the Lord is the beginning of wisdom . . . his praise endureth forever" (111:10).

Jesus' teaching about worship in his conversation with the woman of Samaria (John 4) reveals his insistence on the relation of true worship and vital religion.

Such passages as Acts 2:42 and Colossians 3:16 provide glimpses of the indispensable part played by well-ordered worship in the life of the early church. The Epistles abound with indications of the fact that worship through prayer, Scripture reading, Scripture exposition, and the practice of the ordinances of baptism and the Lord's Supper accounted in a very important measure for the unity, faith, courage, missionary zeal, and effective witnessing of the early church. Volumes have been written on this theme.

Not only do the Scriptures call us to the worship of God and of his Son, our blessed Saviour, but they also warn us against false worship, and the warning is replete with reminders of the eternal tragedy that is bound up with unworthy worship. Exodus 32 presents the abomination of the worship of the golden calf, even while Moses, their leader, seeks to discover the will of the true God on the holy mount of Sinai. Micah 5:13

and Isaiah 2:8, 20 warn men against worshiping the works of their own hands—a form of idolatry which appears altogether too frequently in our own times. In Acts 17:23 we are reminded of the supreme folly of a people who worship "an unknown god"—a noble impulse wrongly directed and woefully starved. The stark penalty of any and all forms of false worship is summed up in the terrifying language of the Apocalypse, "And the smoke of their torment ascendeth up forever and ever: and they have no rest day nor night, who worship the beast and his image, and whosoever receiveth the mark of his name" (Rev. 14:11).

DEFINING WORSHIP

Like all of life's deepest experiences, worship is hard to define in words. The apostle realized this when he exhorted his readers to praise the Lord with "psalms and hymns and spiritual songs" (Col. 3:16; Eph. 5:19). The singer, the poet, and the artist are better equipped to speak of worship than the prose-writer or speaker. The word "worship" is a contraction of the Anglo-Saxon noun "worth-ship." Thus it signifies the recognition of the worth of the object adored. For us it means, then, an act of praise, adoration, thanksgiving, confession, dedication—all based upon our recognition of the "worth" of God. The aged apostle John expresses this in lofty tones when he writes, "Thou art worthy, O Lord, to receive glory and honour and power: for thou hast created all things, and for thy pleasure they are and were created" (Rev. 4:11).

Here we must begin. Worship must be God-centered, not man-centered. The thought and intense desire of the worshiper must be fixed upon God, and not upon self or the concerns of self. Hymns must exalt God and summon the worshipers to glorify him by their lips and in their lives. It is this fact which prompts the rule of thumb that the opening worship hymn in

3

any service must not contain the first personal pronoun! It must focus all thought upon the nature of God—his majesty, power, grace, and love. All the elements of worship must unite to "bless His holy name," and to enable the worshiper to "behold His glory" and to enter into reverent, privileged communication with Him who "is never far from any one of us," yet who dwelleth in heavenly places, which are unapproachable by the feet of men.

Effective worship will accomplish great things for those who wait upon God. It will result in those transformations and controls of thought, feeling, and will without which no one can be and remain a true follower of God and of his Son, Jesus Christ our Lord. Through worship we acknowledge our creatureliness, confess our sins, make due sacrifices of penitence and thanksgiving, present our petitions expectantly before the throne of grace, offer ourselves anew upon the altar of dedication to Almighty God in the name of our Advocate, Jesus Christ (see Rom. 12:1). Through worship we repudiate the claims of the present and "taste the powers of the world to come" (Heb. 6:5). Through worship we commune with God in that glorious two-way encounter dramatized in the Old Testament by the patriarch Jacob's dream of a ladder reaching from earth to heaven, and *from heaven to earth*. Through worship we exercise our sonship with the Father through our adoption in Jesus Christ (Rom. 8:15), seeking to know the Father's will, to share in his work, to be enriched by his boundless generosity, and to pledge him our love and loyalty for time and for eternity. Through worship we achieve vision, insight, faith, devotion and adequacy in ever-increasing measure. "In worship we offer up the whole of our personality, and the fire descends upon the offering," says F. H. Brabant. One might substitute the word "worship" for the word "faith" in the following bit of poetry by Anna E. Hamilton:

4

Faith is a grasping of Almighty power;
The hand of man laid on the arm of God;
The grand and blessèd hour
In which the things impossible to me
Become the possible, O Lord, through thee.

We have been thinking of the worship experience of the individual. Corporate worship, or group worship, is akin to individual worship, for only worshiping individuals can, after all, constitute a worshiping group. On the other hand, there are corporate values and gains in group worship which involve objectives and motivations somewhat different from those defined by the worship of the individual believer. In the worship experience of a group of people the following objectives should be striven for reverently, carefully, creatively:

1. The unification of the group into a fellowship seeking after God with singlehearted purpose and sanctified zeal;

2. The preparation of the mind and heart of the worshipers for a revelation of divine truth and a visitation of transforming power from on high;

3. The assurance to all who worship that "God is, and is the rewarder of them that diligently seek him" (Heb. 11:6);

4. The influencing of all by the sacredness and spirit of the occasion to the point where reverence, quietness, penitence, humility, peace, and expectancy mark the approach of all to Him whom men must worship and adore.

When group worship succeeds in a real measure in meeting these requirements, people are enabled to sing with a glowing sense of reality the words of William Cowper:

Jesus, where'er thy people meet,
There they behold thy mercy-seat:
Where'er they seek thee, thou art found,
And every place is hallowed ground.

5

This book is concerned primarily with group worship and with some readily-used and easily-obtained materials and techniques. It is hoped that with these helps leaders of worship may succeed in transforming disorderly, irreverent, noisy "opening exercises" into services of genuine worship which honor God, uplift his people, disclose his truth, release his healing and saving power, thus enabling the people of our churches, and related organizations, to realize through worship the glorious meaning of the benediction:

> May the grace of the Lord, Jesus Christ, renew your nature;
> May the mercy of God, the Father, cover your sin;
> May the peace of God, the Holy Spirit, crown your joy.

We have dealt somewhat with individual worship simply because group worship in the worthiest sense is impossible apart from worshiping individuals who seek to glorify God.

OBSTACLES TO WORSHIP

Worship "in spirit and in truth" (John 4:23) is next to impossible when the leader's preparation is slovenly and extempore, and when the leader lacks in himself the spirit of humility, reverence, and penitence in the presence of the divine majesty. Too many "worship leaders," falsely so-called, center attention upon themselves rather than upon God in Christ. They seem more concerned that they be honored than that Christ be exalted. They seem more interested in amusing the group than in inspiring them. They seem afraid of quietness and the devotional spirit and aim to make the service "free and easy, bright and breezy." They regard God as a spectator of their efforts, rather than as the sole object of the group's adoration and thoughtful worship. Certainly a careless, egocentric, "slap-happy" leader can make true worship, in the sense in which we have sought to define it, all but impossible. Thus

6

the selection of the right kind of leader, and the cultivation in him—and by him—of the spirit of acceptable worship, are the initial steps in any attempt to improve the quality, atmosphere, and efficacy of the worship of our churches and their organizations.

Other obstacles to worship need only be listed:

1. Unattractive, cluttered-up surroundings

2. Lack of vital co-operation by key people and leaders in the group

3. Lack of the spirit of prayerfulness in the church itself, as a normal atmosphere

4. Lack of elementary equipment and aids to worship, such as curtains, screens, hymnbooks, projector, Bibles, lighting, well-arranged seats, etc.

5. Lack of careful organization involving the selection of suitable people to do necessary things—read, sing, pray, speak, play musical instruments, and many things besides

6. Lack of careful planning of the content and techniques of the services to be held, and of other matters, simple or complex according to the size of the group and the nature of the worship occasion

7. Lack of patient persistence in striving for the spirit of New Testament worship in the face of a backlog of past carelessness, indifference, and neglect

Every obstacle can be overcome by the prayerful, thoughtful, imaginative use of materials within easy reach—the hymnbook, the Bible, poems, stories, simple drama, pictures, silence, and other resources to be mentioned in this book as it develops. The resolve to attain greater skill and effectiveness in the high art of Christian worship is the indispensable factor by which success can be expected. Complacent satisfaction with the present aimless methods will perpetuate the evil of noisy, confused opening exercises, which are an insult to the God whom we are called to worship and an offense to those for whom we have sacred responsibilities as Christian leaders.

After Worship—What?

Succeeding chapters in this book will help to insure careful planning of services of worship. Readily-used guidance is offered for making the service of worship interesting, spiritually and intellectually stimulating, conducive to the proper attitude in the presence of God, and marked by the participation of many in many ways—an end which is much to be desired in Protestant worship where the "priesthood of all believers" should be expressed as well as professed.

Before we proceed to those chapters of practical guidance, let us pause a moment to consider what effective worship should lead to if it is not to become a mystical, pious end in itself, unrelated to the daily opportunities and obligations of the people of God. Worship should illumine our minds with truth, quicken our hearts with love, nerve our wills to high endeavor. In other words, worship should stimulate and motivate us for worthier discipleship and more dynamic crusading for Christ in our world. Cleansed in heart, purified in desire, strengthened in faith, animated with loving concern for all men and for the kingdom of God, we should go out from the place of worship to the places of toil and service better equipped to be "ambassadors of Christ," living witnesses, "read and known of all men." From worship to work, from the meetinghouse to the market place, from devotion to dedicated living—this is the proper progression for the true worshiper, if our profession of the Christian faith is to be confirmed in the practices of our daily lives. Worship must provide the spiritual dynamics for Christlike living amidst the temptations, difficulties, and complexities of a world that seeks to make us "conform" (Rom. 12:2) to its ways, when our calling in Christ is to be "transformed" to his ways.

8

2

The Parts of a Worship Service

AN ANALYSIS OF SOME of the more memorable worship experiences we have had will almost inevitably indicate that they were, in many respects, unconventional. They did not follow the set and stilted pattern too often adhered to. They used materials seldom thought of in more "normal" settings for worship. Let us examine one such worship experience to see how there can be creative departures from familiar worship patterns without any loss of the spirit of reverence and order—indeed, with an enhancement of these very qualities.

This worship experience took place in a bare assembly hall at a boy's camp at the close of a happy and busy camping day. The forty boys and their leaders gathered quietly following the ringing of the camp bell. It was a fixed rule that all conversation cease as campers reached the lodge veranda and before they entered the "house of worship"—for that is what it was to them, verily. A few candles on the fireplace mantle provided the only light in the hall. The boys seated themselves quietly on backless benches arranged along two sides of the hall. In the center floor space eight benches had been arranged in the shape of a cross, four benches for the upright and two for the crossbar. The *theme* of the service was "The Light of the World." The service was as follows:

The *camp director* spoke: "Jesus said, 'I am the light of the world: he that followeth me shall not walk in darkness, but shall have the light of life.'" After about a half-minute of silent prayer, a *quartet* of the boys who had been trained ahead of time sang two stanzas of "The Light of the World Is Jesus."

The *camp director* suggested that they pray together the Lord's Prayer.

Four boys stepped forward and stood about the cross—one at each end of the crossbar, and one at each end of the upright. Each recited a verse of Scripture referring to the light that Jesus is and which his word and truth provide. The *camp director* spoke briefly about our privilege to be a means of shedding the light of Christ into the dark places of human life. The *four boys* about the cross then repeated in unison: "Let your light so shine before men, that they may see your good works, and glorify your Father which is in heaven."

Candles were then distributed to all the boys. A large candle was set in the center of the cross. The leader then requested that every boy who sincerely desired to do so should step forward (no order indicated), light his candle from the large candle symbolizing "the Light of the world," set his candle on the cross (an order having been indicated) in some drops of its own wax, giving a spontaneous word of dedication or witness, such as, "I want my life to shine for Jesus"; or, "I want to walk in the light which Christ sheds upon my way"; or, "I want to dedicate myself to be a light-bearer for Jesus."

All but four of the boys took part in the lighting of the candles and the ensuing act of dedication. *Two older boys* then offered short prayers asking God in Christ to seal the vows which had been taken, and to use every participating boy for the brightening of human life with the light that streams from the cross of Christ.

Electric lights were then turned on, and the *group* sang the hymn "O Master, Let Me Walk with Thee."

10

One need scarcely report that this service left a lasting impression. If one were addicted to alliteration he could say that the service had purpose, participation, progression, and productivity. Analyzing it, we note that it was informal, yet carefully planned. It was very simple in setting, yet utilized symbolism effectively—and by the use of resources close at hand (benches, a fireplace, candles). The service was planned with a response in view. It led somewhere. It brought the boys to a crisis of decision: "What will you do with Jesus?" It was not designed for aesthetic enjoyment merely. It was designed to make a group of boys conscious of the reality of Christ and of the world's need of him, and to make them aware of the fact that he needed them to become his disciples, "light-bearers" in a world of darkness and need.

This service reminds us that the materials and techniques used must be the means, and not the ends, of worship. The true ends have to do with repentance, thanksgiving, awareness, a clear sense of a personal call to service, an overwhelming impulse to say, "Here am I, send me." Lacking these dynamics of spiritual reality, worship services are mere performances, a type of religious exhibitionism.

Note, in the service mentioned, the alternation of music and prayer, of silence and Scripture, of leaders and boys. Such careful, purposeful use of variety, of departure from the familiar and obvious, is to be commended, as long as it is done without sacrifice of reverence and essential dignity.

THE ELEMENTS IN WORSHIP SERVICES

Let us look somewhat more carefully, then, at the elements which should play a part—in various combinations and orders—in effective worship.

In earlier times there was much attention paid to what was known as "the shape of the liturgy," and great pains were often taken to crowd every service, whatever the setting or the occasion, into the fixed liturgical pattern. Nonconformist churches shied away from a tradition which attached almost sacramental significance to the sheer form of a service of worship. Unhappily, the reaction often led to a forfeiture of some real values inherent in a historic liturgical tradition. The "shape of the liturgy" commonly included the following progression of elements:

The praise of God (all worship starts here)

Prayer for purity (consequent upon a viewing of God's majesty and holiness)

The reading of the divine law, and penitence for disobeying it

Seeking the New Testament witness, rich in God's mercy through Christ to sinners

Exhortation and confession (prayers, litanies, meditation, and the like)

The ritual of thanksgiving, for mercy assured and divine promises renewed

Petition for themselves and others (now that the conditions of answered prayer had been fulfilled in the preceding acts of worship)

Certainly some such progression is called for in all worthy worship—from praise to confession, from confession to gratitude, from gratitude to dedication, from dedication to petition. An acrostic which has been very helpful to the writer, as a device for keeping the essential elements of worship in mind, is offered at this point:

A doration (the praise of God's majesty, grace and truth)

C onfession (awakened by the remembrance of who and what God is)

T hanksgiving (for mercies received and promises relied upon)

S upplication (for ourselves and others—really another word for petition)

Remembering this acrostic, based on the word "Acts," will be helpful on many occasions, especially when one is asked—with or without notice—to offer public prayer.

USE OF SUITABLE MATERIALS

The purposeful planning of worship services, in keeping with the principles mentioned, involves, it must be realized, the careful choice and use of suitable materials. Scripture, prayer, and hymn-singing will always be the most vitamin-rich items in any "diet of worship," though their value will consist to an important degree in their appropriateness in furthering the theme chosen to a desired climax. Other items are of much value too, when used wisely. Poems, drama, choral effects, quotations, pictures, and many other readily-obtained aids will occur to creative worship leaders. Yet the following basic rules must be observed in their use if they are to fulfil, rather than frustrate, the purpose of the worship services planned.

1. All materials selected for use must relate closely and obviously to the theme and purpose of the service.

2. All materials should be used reverently, with preparation and conviction. No Scripture passage should be read without preparation, especially by those unaccustomed to reading in public. Mispronounced words, the awkward ignoring of punctuation, and a failure to understand and appreciate what is being read, can detract greatly from the experience of worship and arouse a subtle resentment in the thinking of a group. The same thing applies, of course, to a vocal solo. At least one rehearsal with the accompanist is a must, even if it has to be arranged just before a service, or following a Sunday service prior to the date for which the solo is scheduled. No alibi can suffice for neglect of this. Inexperienced readers, singers, and speakers should have a bit of coaching by a leader—often by the minister himself. "Study to show thyself approved unto

13

God, a workman that needeth not to be ashamed," wrote the apostle Paul; and he wrote it for us!

3. A record of materials used (hymns, solos, poems, and so on) should be kept so that too frequent repetition can be avoided. Good materials should be used frequently, but only with some interval between uses. Variety in the use of beloved familiar material can be achieved by using it in various ways. For example, a hymn sung by the congregation on one occasion may be used as a solo the next time; or a poem used in an address once may be used as a prayer, possibly, the next time. The principle is readily recognized.

4. Handwritten copies of materials may lead to difficulty. Typed or printed copy is always safer—and better for filing. Materials used should be filed by worship leaders for future use, and filed at the church, if at all possible.

5. No material should ever be used as mere "padding." It is much better to omit a poem or a hymn, for example, than to use either without a sense of purpose and with no conviction that it is helpful in furthering the purpose of the service.

These rules may seem elementary and obvious. They are listed for that very reason. When we fail, by carelessness or indolence, to observe the obvious, we are all the more certain to offend our hearers and thus lose influence over them for the furtherance of the gospel.

3

The Call to Worship

THE CALL TO WORSHIP, usually following a quiet musical prelude (to call the group to order), is designed to remind the worshipers of the presence of God, of their own purpose in participating in the worship service, and of the rich possibilities of personal and corporate blessing which worship offers. This opening feature of the service is a summons to reverence, to humility, and to quiet expectation of blessing from the throne of grace.

Calls to worship may be secured from many sources, but the most commonly used materials are: a suitable verse or passage of Scripture; a hymn stanza (read by the leader or by all, or sung by a soloist or by the whole group); a poem, in whole or in part. We list below, from the three sources mentioned, a considerable number of passages which would be suitable as calls to worship. These lists are only illustrative of the wide range of similarly suitable materials which await discovery by the diligent leader.

FROM THE SCRIPTURES

The book of Psalms is the richest treasury in the Bible from which to seek calls to worship. Almost every psalm will provide a verse or more which is suitable for use as a call to worship. Do not be turned aside by the fact that the first two or three

15

verses do not seem to be suitable; the last two or three verses may be unusually so. Consider the following: Psalms 9:1–2; 15:1–2; 16:8–11; 19:1–3, 14; 22:25–27; 24; 25:1–5; 27:1–4; 28:6–9; 31:23–24; 32:1, 10–11; 33:20–22; 34:1–3; 37:3–6; 40: 1–3; 42:1–2; 43:5; 46:1–3; 57:7–11; 63:1–3; 65:1–2; 67; 70: 4–5; 72:17–19; 79:9,13; 84:1–4; 89:1–2, 15–16; 90:1–2; 93; 95:1–3; 96:1–9; 97:1,12; 98:1–4; 100; 103:1–5; 105:1–4; 107: 1–2; 111:1–4; 113:1–3; 116:1,17–19; 118:1, 26–29; 121; 124; 125:1–2; 130:5–6; 138:1–3; 139:7–19; 145:1–5; 146:1–2.

The general requirements for a call to worship are to be discovered in the first reference, Psalm 9:1–2:

> I will give thanks unto the Lord, with my whole heart;
> I will show forth all thy marvelous works.
> I will be glad and exult in thee;
> I will sing praise unto thy name, O thou Most High.

In these words the name of the God we worship is worthily exalted, and expression is given to the desire of the worshiper to praise the Lord and rejoice in his presence.

While a general call to worship is always suitable, it is quite possible to select calls which relate in a striking and memorable way to the theme of the total worship service. For instance, if the theme is "Missions," a striking call to worship would be Isaiah 12:2–6. Or if the theme is "Consecration," Luke 10:27 would serve admirably as a call to worship.

While Psalms, Isaiah, John, and Revelation offer the richest store, other books of the Bible also abound in suitable materials for use as calls to worship. We list below a group of passages which could be used effectively as calls to worship: Exodus 20:24; Deuteronomy 6:5; Isaiah 6:1–8; 15:2–6; 26:1–4; 33:2; 40:9–11, 28–31; 55:1–3; 60:1–3; Jeremiah 7:23; 17:5–7; Micah 6:6–8; Ezekiel 1:28 to 2:2; Matthew 11:28; 18:20; Luke 10:27;

19:37–38; John 1:11–12; 4:4, 23–24; 6:35; 8:12; 10:9–10; 11:25–26; Acts 2:21; Romans 12:1–2; 1 Corinthians 2:9–11; 2 Corinthians 3:17–18; Galatians 1:3–5; Ephesians 1:3–5, 17–18; 3:17–19; Philippians 3:9–11; Hebrews 2:9–10; 4:16; James 4:8a,10; 1 Peter 1:3–5; Revelation 1:10, 12–18; 5:11–13; 7:11; 11:15; 21:6–7.

For effective use of Scripture and hymns together as calls to worship, see the section on hymns.

From the Hymnbook

A great many hymns contain stanzas—one or more—which are suitable to use as calls to worship. In some cases the stanza best suited to this purpose may be the last, rather than the first. Frequently more than one stanza of a hymn should be used. Then again, in calls from the hymnbook which are to be read, only a portion of a stanza may be best for use. Hymnal calls to worship may be either read or sung—read in unison or sung as a solo or by the whole group. The worship leader must give careful thought to the best use of a hymnal call, having in mind the talent he can use from the group and, most of all, the effect he hopes to create by its use. The following hymns will furnish helpful calls to worship (and here again no exhaustive list is attempted), and many others will suggest themselves to thoughtful worship directors.

"All Hail the Power of Jesus' Name"
"Crown Him with Many Crowns"
"Day Is Dying in the West"
"Dear Lord and Father of Mankind"
"Fairest Lord Jesus"
"Holy, Holy, Holy"
"How Sweet the Name of Jesus Sounds"
"Jesus, Thou Joy of Loving Hearts"
"God Reveals His Presence"

17

"Let Us with a Gladsome Mind"
"Lord of All Being, Throned Afar"
"Lord of Our Life and God of Our Salvation"
"O God the Rock of Ages"
"O Love That Wilt Not Let Me Go"
"O Worship the King"
"Praise, My Soul, the King of Heaven"
"Rejoice, the Lord Is King"
"Saviour, Blessed Saviour, Listen While We Sing"
"Spirit of God, Descend upon My Heart"
"Stand Up, and Bless the Lord"
"Strong Son of God, Immortal Love"
"The Lord Is King! Lift Up Thy Voice"
"Thee Will I Love, My Strength and Tower"
"Thou Hidden Source of Calm Repose"
"We Have Not Known Thee as We Ought"
"When All Thy Mercies, O My God"
"Where Cross the Crowded Ways of Life"
"Worship the Lord in the Beauty of Holiness"
"Ye Servants of God, Your Master Proclaim"

In each of the above, stanza 1 is intended, except in the hymn "Stand Up, and Bless the Lord," where stanzas 3 and 4 would be the best choices as calls to worship. Stanza 4 would be effective in the hymn "Ye Servants of God, Your Master Proclaim."

Your choir leader can suggest solos, or portions from great anthems, which also could be used—read or sung—as calls to worship.

Where it is desired to use a hymnal call to worship which is not in the hymnary available to the group, the selected stanza can be written on the blackboard and read in unison, or sung, by the group. It is also quite easy to have a lantern slide made of a stanza so that it can be read or sung from the screen as the worship period opens. If other material happens to be mimeographed for use during the worship service, the call to worship should then, of course, be included with such material, and sung or read from the mimeographed sheets handed out at the door as the worshipers entered.

FROM POETRY

Many short stanzas of poetry serve admirably as calls to worship. After all, most hymns are poems, and many poems might well be put to music and used as hymns. Consider the following poetic calls to worship as suggestive of the great number to be discovered by the industrious leader.

> My soul leans toward Him; stretches out its arms,
> And waits expectant. Speak to me, my God:
> And let me know the living Father cares
> For me, even me; for this one of His children.
> God, let Thy mighty heart beat into mine,
> And let mine answer as a pulse of Thine.
>
> GEORGE MACDONALD

> To crowds that throng the city streets,
> Or jostle in the marts of trade;
> To careless youth whose joyous feet
> Dance through the world that Thou hast made;
> To masters in the realms of thought,
> And toilers all, beneath the rod;
> To lonely hearts by men forgot,
> Be this to each—the House of God.
>
> GEORGE A. LEICHLITER

> Yea, through life, death, through
>   sorrow and through sinning,
> Christ shall suffice me, for He hath sufficed;
> Christ is the end, for Christ was the beginning,
> Christ the beginning, for the end is Christ.
>
> F. W. H. MYERS

Trembling before Thee, we fall down to adore Thee,
Shamefaced and trembling we lift our hearts to Thee,
O First and with the last!
Full of pity view us, stretch Thy sceptre to us,
Bid us live that we may give ourselves to Thee:
O faithful Lord and true; stand up for us, and lo,
Make us lovely, make us new, set us free,
Heart and soul and spirit to bring all and worship Thee.

CHRISTINA ROSSETTI

Lord, what a change within us one short hour
Spent in Thy presence can avail to make!
What heavy burdens from our bosoms take,
What parchéd grounds refresh as with a shower!
We kneel, and all around us seems to lower;
We rise, and all, the distant and the near,
Stands forth in sunny outline brave and clear;
We kneel, how weak! we rise, how full of power!
Why, therefore, should we do ourselves this wrong,
Or others, that we are not always strong,
That we are ever overborne with care,
That we should ever weak or heartless be,
Anxious or troubled, when with us is prayer,
And joy and strength and courage are with Thee!

ARCHBISHOP TRENCH

In the excellent anthology of religious poetry, *Masterpieces of Religious Verse,* edited by James Dalton Morrison and published by Harper & Brothers, there are, among more than 2000 poems, many that lend themselves for use as calls to worship. Those who have this valuable volume might well consider the following for use as calls to worship:

"Thou Life Within My Life" ....No. 108
"Lord, Who Art Merciful" 120
"Eternal God! O Thou that Only Art" 142
"The All-Loving" 154

"The Search for God" 166
"Great Art Thou, O Lord" 198
"Wait On" 208
"Delight in God Only" 219
"God Makes a Path" 241
"God of Our Life" 311
"Thy Glory Alone, O God" 356
"The Marshes of Glynn" (extract) 357
"Awareness" 396

Another valuable collection of religious verse is *1000 Quotable Poems,* compiled by Thomas Curtis Clark, and obtainable from all book stores. The following poems from that collection should be considered for use as calls to worship:

"The World Is Too Much With Us" ....P.   8
"Chartless" 24
"Credo" 29–30
"In Thy Presence" 53
"Sanctuary" 58
"Windows of the Soul" 80
"Acceptance" 106
"I Know a Name" 146
"A Hymn for the New Age" 178

Single stanzas or longer portions are to be used according to the leader's judgment.

Suitable poetic calls to worship often will be found in magazines, church school papers, and elsewhere in one's general reading. Copies of all should be made and filed carefully under topics.

HYMNS AND POEMS COMBINED

Distinctive worship values are achieved through a careful combination of hymn and poem stanzas of kindred theme. Any volume of religious verse—of which many will be found in any good book store—will offer, in well-indexed form, a fine array of topics such as are used frequently in worship services by church groups. Poems abound on such fundamental themes as: Christ, the church, faith, love, prayer, brotherhood, the cross, missions, special days in the church year, and so forth. In addition to the volumes already specified, let us suggest *The World's Great Religious Poetry* by Caroline Hill (Macmillan Co.) and *Poems of Justice* by Thomas Curtis Clark (Willett, Clark and Co.).

Consider the following call to worship as an illustration of this interesting possibility of verse and hymn combination:

LEADER (*or choral-reading group of three to six*): Luke 12: 22–32

VOICE FROM AUDIENCE (*reader stands at his place*):

> Lord, give me faith!—to live from day to day,
> With tranquil heart to do my simple part,
> And, with my hand in thine, just go Thy way.
>
> Lord, give me faith!—to trust, if not to know;
> With quiet mind in all things Thee to find,
> And, child-like, go where Thou wouldst have me go.
>
> JOHN OXENHAM

HYMN: "Lord, for Tomorrow and Its Needs"
LEADER: Romans 8:28, 31
READER:

> I will not doubt, though all my ships at sea
> Come drifting home with broken masts and sails;
> I shall believe the Hand which never fails,
> From seeming evil worketh good to me;
> And, though I weep because those sails are battered,

22

Still will I cry, while my best hopes lie shattered,
    "I trust in Thee."
ELLA WHEELER WILCOX

GROUP (*in unison*): Acts 27:21–25
HYMN: "I Heard the Voice of Jesus Say," or, "Immortal Love, Forever Full"
SILENT PRAYER
VOICE (*slowly*):

O Maker of the Mighty Deep
Whereon our vessels fare,
Above our life's adventure keep
Thy watchful love and care.
In Thee we trust, whate'er befall;
Thy sea is great, our boats are small.
HENRY VAN DYKE

The Lord's Prayer in unison concludes this service—one which obviously would be suitable for a New Year occasion.

This use of hymn and poem combined makes a somewhat elaborate call to worship, and might even be regarded as a brief, complete *service* of worship, rather than a *call*. Such classification relates to the length and purpose of the worship planned.

Once more let it be stressed that all parts should be carefully taken by persons who do so reverently, conscientiously, and in clear and expressive voice. Much usable material is easy to find, but consecrated care is needed to use it to the best advantage in the interest of worship experiences rich in the values which God desires.

It is an excellent idea for any church organization to have on hand for reference several hymnals from various publishers other than the book commonly used by the congregation. Every good hymnary has some hymns copyrighted for that volume. A variety of hymns, familiar and unfamiliar, is valuable for solos, calls to worship, prayers, responses, and so forth. All good book stores carry a list of hymnals from various publishers, and will order any which are not in their stocks. It is wise to make a note of the names and publishers of books you come upon as you travel, visit, and partake in church gatherings beyond your local church.

DEVOTIONAL BOOKS

Many familiar devotional books contain calls to worship and other materials suitable for use in the planning of worship services. Such well-known booklets as *Open Windows, The Upper Room, The Secret Place,* and *Today* contain poems, worshipful quotations, and Scripture passages which would serve well as calls to worship.

The following bound volumes of well-tested books are rich in worship materials:

Lyric Religion, by H. Augustine Smith (Westwood, N. J.: Fleming H. Revell Co., 1931), is a rich source of material on hymns.

God's Minute (Philadelphia, Pa.: John C. Winston Co.) has 365 short prayers (one a day).

The Glory of God, by Georgia Harkness (Nashville, Tennessee: Abingdon Press, 1943), has many fine devotional poems and prayers.

Open the Meeting with Prayer, by Alfred Doerffler (St. Louis, Missouri: Concordia Publishing House), has many prayers grouped under useful headings.

Your denominational book store can secure any of these for you on order.

4

Making the Most of Hymns

CHRISTIANITY IS A singing faith. In no other religion does music play so great a part in the worship and witness of all the people. The apostle Paul, writing to the Colossians, said, "Let the word of Christ dwell in you richly in all wisdom; teaching and admonishing one another in psalms and hymns and spiritual songs, singing with grace in your hearts to the Lord" (3:16). The word "teaching" should be underscored, because hymns represent one of Christianity's most effective means of instruction in doctrine and in the principles of Christian conduct day by day. Perhaps second only to the Bible itself, the hymnbook is a manual of training in the discipline, joy, and responsibility of the follower of the Master.

Of great hymns it may well be said, in Longfellow's words:

> Such songs have power to quiet
> The restless pulse of care,
> And come like the benediction
> That follows after prayer.

It need scarcely be emphasized here that the value deriving from the use of good hymns depends not only on a wise selection of the hymns, but also upon a thoughtful, hearty singing by those present. The singing rules of John Wesley are

25

as timely now as they were when he made such effective use of hymn singing in his great evangelistic services long ago.

1. Learn the tune.
2. Sing the words as they are printed.
3. Sing lustily and with a good courage.
4. All sing. "If it is a cross to you, take it up and you will find a blessing."
5. Sing in time. Do not run before or stay behind.
6. Above all, sing spiritually. Have an eye to God in every word you sing. Aim at pleasing Him more than yourself or any other creature. Attend strictly to the sense of what you sing, and see that your heart is not carried away with the sound, but offered to God continually.

Varied Uses of Hymns

Thoughtlessness and carelessness in the use of hymns are all too common faults of worship leaders. Too few realize the values to be gained from the skilful use of the hymnbook. In this chapter we hope to demonstrate that it is quite easy for any average church leader to use hymns in ways which will bring pleasure, inspiration, and guidance to worshipers young and old. Hymn stanzas may be well employed in relation to almost any part of a worship service.

Hymns as Calls to Worship

Many hymn stanzas constitute strong calls to worship. They may be used in a variety of ways. A soloist may sing a call quietly and unaccompanied from the back of the meeting room. The group in charge of a meeting may march in a processional to seats at the front of the room, singing a call to worship as they do so. The hymnal call may be written on a blackboard, shown as a slide on a screen, or mimeographed for use by the whole group standing.

Hymns suitable for use as calls to worship include the following:

"God Reveals His Presence" (stanza 1)
"Glory Be to God the Father" (stanzas 1 and 4)
"Jesus, Stand Among Us in Thy Risen Power" (all stanzas)
"Jesus, Thou Joy of Loving Hearts" (stanzas 1 and 4)
"Jesus, Wondrous Saviour" (any of the stanzas)
"Lord of All Being, Throned Afar" (stanza 1; 3 and 4 together)
"Praise to the Lord, the Almighty" (stanza 1)
"Praise, My Soul, the King of Heaven" (stanza 1)
"Worship the Lord in the Beauty of Holiness" (stanza 1, or all stanzas)

A somewhat elaborate, but easily-arranged, use of the hymn call may take the form of a pantomime. For example, a worship service could be effectively introduced by a pantomimic representation of the hymn "Praise, My Soul, the King of Heaven."
A concealed soloist, or group of singers, sings the hymn as several girls, dressed in white, appear on the platform and make the gestures indicated below:

SOLOIST: "Praise, My Soul, the King of Heaven,"
PANTOMIMISTS *clasp hands beneath chins, gazing heavenward.*
SOLOIST: "To His feet thy tribute bring;"
PANTOMIMISTS *kneel on one knee, and, with heads bowed, hold hands forward as if laying gifts on the floor just in front of them.*
SOLOIST: "Ransomed, healed, restored, forgiven,"
PANTOMIMISTS *gather in semi-circle around a table behind where they have been standing, and lay hands on an open Bible, looking at it with happy expressions because of the Gospel it declares.*
SOLOIST: "Who like me His praise should sing?"
PANTOMIMISTS *step forward, arms flung wide apart, heads turned*

upward, mouths open as though singing joyously toward heaven.

SOLOIST: "Praise Him, praise Him, praise Him, praise Him, Praise the everlasting King."

PANTOMIMISTS *join hands in circle, kneel to one knee and turn faces upward as though beholding a vision splendid.*

(*Lights dim out as the singer finishes the stanza, and the voice of the leader is heard saying: "O come and worship the Lord with me, and let us exalt His name together.*")

Hymns Used with Scripture Reading

The co-ordination of hymn stanzas and Scripture passages presenting the same theme is very effective, the Scripture interpreting the meaning of the hymn more fully, and the hymn throwing added light upon the Scripture used. A Scripture passage may be read by a reader, after which the entire group sings the stanza(s) announced, stimulating all who hear to practice in their daily lives the word which has come to them through the reading of the Scriptures. Suitable stanzas for this purpose are:

"Break Thou the Bread of Life" (stanza 2)
"Jesus, Thou Joy of Loving Hearts" (stanza 2)
"Lead Us, O Father, in the Paths of Peace" (stanza 2)
"Lord, Thy Word Abideth" (stanza 1, or any of the others)

As an alternative a soloist may sing the hymn stanza, after which the group reads the interpretive Scripture passage in unison. Typical hymns of this type are: "Break Thou the Bread of Life"; "Father of Mercies, in Thy Word"; "Lord, Speak to Me, That I May Speak"; "O Word of God Incarnate"; "Teach Me, O Lord, the Perfect Way"; "That Man Hath Perfect Blessedness"; "The Heavens Declare Thy Glory, Lord"; "The Spirit Breathes upon the Word."

The following illustrations of this readily-arranged treatment serve to illustrate further how easily a leader may use similar material from the Bible and the hymnbook. Practice in the use of a Bible concordance and a hymnbook index will help.

"How Firm a Foundation"
ALL SING: Stanza 1 ("How firm a foundation")
LEADER READS: 1 Corinthians 3:9–11
ALL SING: Stanza 2 ("Fear not, I am with thee;")
LEADER: 1 Corinthians 10:12–13
ALL SING: Stanza 3 ("When through the deep waters")
LEADER: Hebrews 12:1–6, or vv. 3–6
ALL SING: Stanza 4 ("When through fiery trials")
LEADER: 2 Corinthians 12:8–11
ALL SING: Stanza 5 ("The soul that on Jesus")
LEADER: Luke 11:9–13

The order could be reversed with equally good effect, the leader reading first, followed in each case by the group-singing of the stanza called for.

"Come, Let Us Sing of a Wonderful Love"
LEADER: John 3:16–18
ALL SING: Stanza 1 ("Come, let us sing of a wonderful love")
LEADER: Luke 4:16–19
ALL SING: Stanza 2 ("Jesus the Saviour this gospel to tell")
LEADER: Matthew 23:37–39
ALL SING: Stanza 3 ("Jesus is seeking the wanderers yet")
LEADER: John 21:15–17
ALL SING: Stanza 4 ("Come to my heart, O thou wonderful Love")

Provision could be made for more participation by group members in an effective service if four young people stood on the platform and, in turn, recited the passages given, with the group singing in response as indicated. If this is to be most effective, the passages should be memorized by the participants rather than read from Bibles in their hands. This is "functional memorizing," that is, memorization related to a specific service for the Master. It is a type of memorization which brings particular satisfaction to the memorizer and benefit to those before whom it is recited.

The great hymn "Dear Lord and Father of Mankind" is used very helpfully with Scripture as follows:

> Stanza 1, followed by the reading of John 4:23
> Stanza 2, followed by the reading of Mark 1:17–18
> Stanza 3, followed by the reading of Mark 1:35
> Stanza 4, followed by the reading of Philippians 4:7
> Stanza 5, followed by the reading of 1 Kings 19:12–13

A hymnic Scripture lesson using "The Son of God Goes Forth to War" is suggested below, and illustrates the ease with which similar treatments could be arranged for many familiar hymns and beloved Scripture passages:

> ALL SING: Stanza 1 ("The Son of God goes forth to war")
> LEADER: Acts 7:54–55
> ALL SING: Stanza 2 ("The martyr first, whose eagle eye")
> LEADER: Hebrews 11:33–38
> ALL SING: Stanza 3 ("A glorious band, the chosen few")
> LEADER: Revelation 7:13–15
> ALL SING: Stanza 5 ("A noble army, men and boys")

One half of the group could sing, the other half responding by unison reading from Bibles.

Hymns Used with Interpretive Poems

There is no end to the possibilities of using hymns and poems together. A poem on social justice could be integrated with such a hymn as "Where Cross the Crowded Ways of Life," or, "Lead On, O King Eternal." A poem on God in nature could be used with such hymns as "For the Beauty of the Earth," "The Spacious Firmament on High," "Fairest Lord Jesus," and many others. The collections of verse already referred to are filled with poems which might be used in this manner. H. Augustine Smith's excellent book *Lyric Religion* contains many treatments of this type, usable in average church situations. This book is to be highly commended as a source book for worship leaders.

Here is an illustrative treatment of hymn and poems used together for worship purposes, employing a well-known missionary hymn, "We've a Story to Tell to the Nations."

LEADER: Hear a short poem written of India by a devoted Canadian Baptist missionary, the late Dr. John Bates McLaurin:

> Lord, make this ancient land thine own;
>   Send forth thy word from sea to sea,
> That these wide fields, in weeping sown,
>   May yield a harvest vast for thee.
>
> God save her people! Through the night
>   Of sin and want they seek Thy face;
> O do Thou dawn upon their sight,
>   And guide them to Thy throne of grace.
>
> Claim, then, this land's devotion, Lord,
>   Her sons' and daughters' fervent love—
> The children's prayers to idols poured,
>   O may they reach Thy throne above.
>
> Pour out on them Thy spirit, Lord,
>   In ocean fullness, mercy free;
> Fulfil Thy will and speak Thy word,
>   And turn this people's heart to Thee.

ALL SING: "We've a Story to Tell to the Nations" (*stanza 1*).

LEADER: On the occasion of Queen Victoria's Diamond Jubilee in June, 1897, the famed British poet Rudyard Kipling wrote the powerful poem, now a hymn, "Recessional." It summons men to realize that true greatness in men and nations is not in armaments and authority, but in humility and the graces of the Christian character. Hear a stanza from this great jubilee poem:

> The tumult and the shouting dies;
> The captains and the kings depart—
> Still stands Thine ancient Sacrifice,
> An humble and a contrite heart.
> Lord God of Hosts, be with us yet,
> Lest we forget—lest we forget!

ALL SING: "We've a song to be sung to the nations" (*stanza 2*).

LEADER: Christina Rossetti wrote this deeply devotional prayer-poem:

> Use me, God, in Thy great harvest field,
> Which stretcheth far and wide like a wide sea;
> The gatherers are so few; I fear the precious yield
> Will suffer loss. Oh, find a place for me!
> A place where best the strength I have will tell;
> It may be one the older toilers shun;
> Be it a wide or narrow place, 'tis well
> So that the work it holds be only done.

ALL SING: "We've a message to give to the nations" (*stanza 3*).

LEADER: The Saviour has committed to his church the task of bearing the gospel to all nations. Once more through poetry we are reminded, in the words of Dr. Thomas B. McDormand, of the spirit Christ's church must show in these years of unrivaled opportunity and difficulty.

O Church of Christ, arise to grasp
 The sceptre of thy sovereignty;
Go forth Christ's Kingdom now to claim
 O'er far-flung continent and sea.

Go forth with banners skyward flung,
 With dauntless faith, and courage high;
Assured that with your forces go
 The powers that rule the earth and sky.

Lay forthright claim to human life
 In fealty to a Father's love;
Possess the Kingdoms of the world
 For Him who reigneth from above.

ALL SING: "We've a Saviour to show to the nations" (*stanza 4*).
PRAYER: A brief period of silent prayer, followed by audible prayers in which several members of the group pray for mission fields and missionaries by name. (*Prayer cards, containing objects of petition, may be handed to several members as they enter the room before the service, and used, in the order in which they have been numbered, for the prayers thus offered.*)

Hymns Used with Great Religious Pictures

A very impressive worship service can be built around a great religious picture, displayed either with a lantern slide, or by means of a good-sized inexpensive print set on an easel on a table at the front of the room. In the latter case the picture should be placed over the mouth of a cardboard box containing a strong electric bulb or else so placed as to be in the focus of a good spotlight. The use of hymns in such a service is illustrated in the following arrangement of material related to the picture "The Light of the World."

CALL TO WORSHIP: "In the beginning was the Word, and the Word was with God, and the Word was God. . . . In him was life; and the life was the light of men. . . . That was the true Light, which lighteth every man that cometh into the world."

(The picture is unveiled on the easel, lights being turned low as this is done. A spotlight already is focused on the picture, unless a lantern screen is used. A period of quiet meditative viewing of the picture follows for at least an entire minute.)

INSTRUMENTAL MUSIC *(softly by violin or piano)*: "The Light of the World Is Jesus," two stanzas only. *(Then a vocal soloist sings the first stanza only.)*

SCRIPTURE READING *(by one or two readers)*: Luke 2:25–32; John 8:12; 9:4–5

PRAYER *(accompanied by soft playing of "O Love That Wilt Not Let Me Go." As silent or audible prayer ends, soloist sings softly, as heads remain bowed, the second stanza of the hymn.)*

HYMN: "When We Walk with the Lord"

Note: Often there is an interesting story related to the painting of a great work of religious art, or concerning a spiritual experience of the painter. In such cases the story might well be told as the picture is unveiled. Many books have been written on religious art and can be supplied by your book store. Alice Anderson Bays, in her book *Worship Programs in the Fine Arts* (Cokesbury), provides helpful material of this type. It should also be remembered that there are many fascinating and inspiring stories about hymns and hymn writers. These stories often can be told in introducing a hymn. *Famous Stories of Inspiring Hymns* by E. K. Emurian (W. A. Wilde and Co.) is a worth-while book of this type.

Hymns Used as Prayers

It is often valuable to use a suitable hymn stanza as a call to prayer or, following the prayer, as a response thereto.

Suitable calls to prayer are furnished by such hymns as:

> "From Every Stormy Wind That Blows"
> "What a Friend We Have in Jesus"
> "Breathe on Me, Breath of God"
> "O Breath of God, Breathe on Us Now"
> "Spirit of God, Descend upon My Heart"
> "Lord, Thy Mercy Now Entreating"

Some suitable responses to use at the conclusion of a prayer are:

> "Breathe on Me, Breath of God"   1144898
> "Gracious Spirit, Dwell with Me"
> "Dear Lord and Father of Mankind"
> "O Lord and Master of Us All"
> "Lead, Kindly Light"
> "O Love That Wilt Not Let Me Go"
> "Lead Us, O Father, in the Paths of Peace"

Such hymn responses can be sung by the whole group or by a soloist; or can be read by the chairman or in unison by all. In most cases one stanza will serve this purpose.

Hymns Used with the Offertory

The singing of a suitable hymn stanza before or after the offering is received can have great value in adding worshipful significance to the act of giving. In some cases a Scripture command is read as the offering is announced, and a hymn stanza sung, with the congregation standing, as the offering is brought to the altar.

This list is illustrative of hymns suitable for offering use:

"We Give Thee But Thine Own" (stanza 1)
"Take My Life and Let It Be" (stanza 4)
"When I Survey the Wondrous Cross" (stanza 4)
"As with Gladness Men of Old" (stanza 3)
"All Things Are Thine" (stanza 1)
"Bless Thou the Gifts" (stanza 1)

A particularly suitable stanza for use before the offering, to be sung from memory by the group with heads bowed, is this (to the tune of "Evening Prayer"):

> Grant us, Lord, the grace of giving,
> With a spirit large and free,
> That ourselves and all our living
> We may offer unto Thee. Amen.

A careful study of a good hymnal will reveal many more stanzas of value for offertory purposes. The few mentioned are familiar, and easily used.

Hymns in Special Services

A well-planned use of hymns on special occasions can do much to lead the group into the very presence of God with hearts prepared for a worship experience. In fact, occasionally a service for a special occasion may be built entirely around suitable hymns, using such Scripture, story, poetry, and comment as may heighten the value derived from the use of the hymns.

1. CHRISTMAS

A Christmas service might well be arranged in relation to the fact that Christmas is internationally loved and celebrated. Such a service could use carols of different nations, interspersed with suitable Scripture, pantomimes or tableaux, lantern slides, prayer, and comment. Among others the following Christmas hymns could be used:

36

"O Come, All Ye Faithful" (Latin)
"Silent Night, Holy Night" (Austrian)
"O Little Town of Bethlehem" (American)
"O Come, O Come, Emmanuel" (English)
"In a Manger He Is Lying" (Polish)
"When Christ Was Born on Earth" (Italian)
"Christmas Brings Joy to Every Heart" (Danish)
"Angels We Have Heard on High" (French)
"O Fir Tree Dark, O Fir Tree Dear" (Swedish)
"Today the Drooping Hearts Find Gladness" (Icelandic)

In using this type of service, it would be interesting to relate briefly Christmas customs followed in some of the lands in which the carols were written. Two or three national ways of observing Christmas we mention.

Sweden.—In Sweden it is believed that on Christmas Eve the ancestors come back to their farmhouses and cottages— not in a ghostly way, but as fragrant memories. The tables are laid for them and beds made. The real inhabitants behave as though they are intruders who are getting a night's lodging there. On the table is found a heap of Christmas cakes called *julhog.* On the bottom is the *julkuse,* a large cake beautifully decorated; next comes the ring cross, or wheel, with four spokes, representing the sun. The two horizontal spokes represent east and west on the earth, and the vertical ones the sun's light and the earth's vegetation. On top of the *julhog* is the golden wagon—four crossed scrolls—the ancient symbol of the god Thor. Contrary to expectation, these breads are not eaten at Christmas, but are saved until spring.

The Christmas season officially opens on December 13, as St. Lucy, dressed in white and wearing a green crown with lighted candles on it, awakens the members of the household by bringing them coffee and cake on a tray. Rice cooked in milk, decorated with cinnamon and having in it one almond, is, even today, served on Christmas Eve. The one who finds the almond first will be the first to marry. No one is served who does not first recite a rhyme. Gifts are opened on Christmas Eve around the family tree. Funny rhymes are written on the wrappers of the packages, describing what they contain without naming it. It is said that goats of straw were the first gifts Sweden made for its children.

France.—Christmas begins in France with the planting of St. Barbara's grain on the fourth of December. Two or three plates are filled with wheat floating in water and placed on the warm ashes of the fireplace or in a sunny window to sprout the grain. If it grows well, there will be a bounteous harvest. The twelve days preceding Christmas foretell the weather for the twelve months to come. If Christmas falls on Friday, even that which is sown in ashes will grow, and harvest will be bountiful.

The yule log is known as *cacho-fio*. The whole family must take part in bringing it in. It is taken from a fruit-bearing tree, usually an almond or olive. Olive trees are considered sacred, and it is believed that lightning never strikes them. An apple or pear tree will also serve the purpose, and up in the Alps region oaks are used. There is a shout of joy as the tree falls. The log should be large enough to last from Christmas Eve until the evening of New Year's Day. Each night it is smothered in ashes. The logs of the poor people are only large enough to last over Christmas Day, and those of the very poor can with care only be made to burn until midnight. The log is to be treated with respect inasmuch as it is considered a harbinger of blessing. Its ashes added to medicine make it more potent. Sprinkled in chicken houses and cow stables, the ashes ward off disease; set in a clothes closet, they are an unfailing protection against fire.

Nougat, turkey, and cake are the important items on a Christmas menu.

The now familiar creche is made of molasses, lichens, laurel, holly, and pasteboard. It is said to have been invented by St. Francis of Assisi. When completed it includes all the characters which appear in the story of the Nativity, the last ones added being the three kings. On Christmas Eve the lighting of the creche candle precedes even the laying of the yule log. The yule log is carried in by the youngest and the oldest members of the family.

The memories of a glad Christmas to a burdened heart are like crumbs of Christmas bread carried by sailors to strew on troubled waters.

Lantern slides of great masterpieces of religious art by artists of various nations could be used very effectively with carols from such nations. The list of masterpieces indicates this possibility:

"Madonna and Child," by Giotto (Italian)
"Adoration of the Magi," by Velasquez (Spanish)
"Virgin and Child," by Van Dyck (Flemish)
"The Arrival of the Shepherds," by Lerolle (French)
"Adoration of the Magi," by Durer (German)

Suitable Christmas poems could well be used at intervals through such a service as suggested. December issues of magazines, Sunday school papers, and church periodicals furnish suggestions.

A fine little introductory poem for a Christmas service is that written by Edward Cooper Mason and appearing in a Sunday school paper a few years ago:

O golden cycle of the year,
That marks the Saviour's birth!
Carols of praise, good will, good cheer,
Spread gladness o'er the earth.

39

The spirit of the Christ-Child comes
With all its glorious thrall,
To brighten all our earthly homes
And tell God's love to all.

And the service could close by the recitation from the back of the room of W. L. Stidger's little poem "The Christmas Song" (also set to music):

The world's wild heart is hushed tonight
Before a Baby's cry—
The shepherds in the field have seen
A strange light in the sky.
A mother's soul is singing there
Before a Manger throne.
But on that dawn three Wise Men met
As meets the world today—
In brotherhood and reverence
To kneel and love and pray.
A star, a song, a dream, a hope,
A prophecy's long quest;
A mother's love, a child's sweet smile,
And all God's world is blest.

Follow the recitation with the choir humming one stanza of "Hark! the Herald Angels Sing."

And after such a carol as "It Came upon the Midnight Clear," have a moment of silent prayer, accompanied after a moment by the reading of this little poem of William Lytles:

Have you any old grudge you would like to pay,
Any wrong laid up from a bygone day?
Gather them now and lay them away
    When Christmas comes.
Hard thoughts are heavy to carry, my Friend,
And life is short from beginning to end;
Be kind to yourself, leave nothing to mend
    When Christmas comes.

Such a carol service will be enhanced by the introduction of such variety as is made possible by the use of a junior choir in the gallery (or at the back of the church), soloist, quartets, all supported in planned ways by the congregation.

2. EASTER

Easter is uniquely a time for praise, and song is the supreme language of praise. The joy of life triumphing over death, of light conquering the darkness, of Christ sealing his triumph over the forces of evil—these are resounding themes of Easter. In spirit and in truth the Christian at Easter can fulfil the exhortation of the psalmist: "O sing unto Jehovah a new song; for he hath done marvellous things: his right hand, and his holy arm, hath wrought salvation for him."

An Easter service of great value can easily be planned around the use of some great hymns.

(*At the opening of the service three women or girls, dressed in dark clothing with dark scarves or shawls on their heads, kneel before a tomblike entrance—made of building paper and marked with black chalk or crayon to resemble rock. Lights are very dim in the church. As the procession of singers reaches the front of the church, the three women will rise, turn toward the audience with happy faces, then hurry off the platform as though seeking the risen Christ. The procession of singers is led by four Junior girls, each carrying a potted Easter lily. As the singers line up on either side of the tomb, the lilies will be placed on the floor across the open door of the tomb.*)

SOLO (*from behind the tomb*): "O Come and Mourn with Me Awhile" (*two stanzas*)

READER: Acts 2:22–23

PRAYER: of penitence for the sins which crucified Christ, and a plea for the forgiveness of those who in our time crucify Christ by sin, indifference, and neglect

PROCESSION (*from the side or rear of the church*): "Jesus Christ Is Risen Today." (*Congregation rises and joins in singing of the last stanza.*)

READERS (*Four dressed in white, carrying similar types of Bible, march to the platform—two from each side or all from the tomb entrance—and read in unison*): Luke 24:1-6.

SOLO (*from the back of the room*): "Crown Him" (*two stanzas*)

ADDRESS: on the new life that comes to men's hearts when they admit the crucified Christ, and the world's need of our faithful proclamation of the gospel of a crucified, risen, and glorified Christ (*The processional group then marches off the platform singing "Crown Him with Many Crowns," and takes its place, still standing, at reserved seats at the front of the church. The congregation then rises and sings the last stanza or two of the hymn with the choir.*)

POEM (*read by a young person*):

How brave that man of Nazareth!
The Son of Man, the Son of God;
When, faced with pain, and scorn, and shame
He faltered not—and, heart aflame,
He bore the Cross; and, with last breath
Spoke love for those who caused His death.

For one like Him there had to be
An Easter morn, a triumph day—
For, love like His death could not know—
The grave must let its victim go;
And all mankind the Christ must see—
Killed, buried, risen—Glad Victory!

THOMAS BRUCE McDORMAND

SCRIPTURE: Romans 6:3-11
SOLO: "Jesus, the Crucified, Pleads for Me"

SILENT PRAYER

HYMN (*by all*): "The Day of Resurrection," or "Hail, Thou Once Despised Jesus"

CLOSING PRAYER

CHOIR: "Holy, Holy, Holy" (*stanza 2*)

Hymns Accompanied by Dramatic Features

Splendid effects often are secured by the use with hymns of easy dramatic devices, such as pantomimes and tableaux. By way of illustration, we reproduce the following dramatization to accompany "In the Cross of Christ I Glory."

Fix a large cross at center back. Place back of it an elevation for the Spirit of the Cross to stand on.

LIGHTING:

> *First Stanza:* Light amber throughout
> *Second Stanza:* Darkening through red to deep lavender
> *Third Stanza:* Specially placed light turned on by the suppliant at the word "Light"
> *Fourth Stanza:* White growing brighter through to end

CHARACTERS AND COSTUMES:

> The *Suppliant:* in lavender, being careful to avoid connotations of angels or Greek maidens
> The *Spirit of the Cross:* in white
> *Woes of Life:* draped in deep purple, with black crepe over shoulder

ACTION:

> Hymn is played through. During the playing the Spirit of the Cross takes her place back of the cross.
> *First Stanza:* Suppliant enters. Kneels before the cross. End of the stanza finds her arms lifted, indicating exultation.

43

Second Stanza: Suppliant gradually relaxes and sinks to floor. Lowest point at close of stanza. Woes of Life enters, places black cape on Suppliant. She vainly attempts to raise her arms in prayer as before.

Third Stanza: Spirit of the Cross leaves her position, comes down, removes black cape and lets it fall on the floor. Suppliant begins to show joy.

Fourth Stanza: Suppliant very gradually raises arms again. She has been sitting low; now she rises to knee position. Spirit of the Cross takes position again. Fullest light, highest position by the end of the last stanza.

Hymn played through again. Lights out. Characters exit.

Using Interesting Facts About Hymns

The use of interesting facts about hymns can do much to increase the enjoyment and value of the singing of the hymns. For example, the writer saw a simple dramatization of the events leading up to the writing of "Abide with Me," by Dr. Francis Lyte. The dramatization had been written by a young lady and was based on the biographical note concerning Dr. Lyte which appeared in Kathleen Blanchard's book *Stories of Popular Hymns.* Following the heart-touching dramatization, the hymn was sung with deep feeling and fine effect by a group of young people.

Such simple dramatization could be prepared in connection with almost any familiar hymn about whose author something is known.

To mention an interesting fact about a hymn or hymn writer, in announcing the use of the hymn, will often add much to the interest and enjoyment with which the congregation sings. For instance, although much of our music is national in origin, international folk songs form the background for many of our hymn tunes. This information, supplied in more detail by any hymnal index, would furnish a splendid basis for an interesting missionary or international good will service.

The suitability of using for a youth service hymns by youthful hymn writers can be seen readily. Facts about hymns written by laymen in various occupations might be worked into a Labor Day service, or one for Layman's Day observance. Another interesting group consists of hymns written specifically for children.

Facts of interest in regard to hymns may be found in Augustine Smith's book *Lyric Religion*.

From the foregoing treatment of the use of hymns, it is apparent that leaders of worship in churches and church organizations can, by the use of more time and care, do much to make possible for their people of all ages greater enjoyment and profit in the use of their hymnal. Variety, with dignity and insight, should be the objective of leaders in their employment of hymns for worship. We urge the importance of teaching new ones. Every beloved and familiar hymn was new once. New hymns learned may be a means of grace to many. Consider, for example, such comparatively new songs as "Come, Let Us Sing of a Wonderful Love," "Spirit of God, Descend upon My Heart." How richly God has blessed their use!

It should be pointed out that the subject index of a hymnal will not always direct us to all the hymns we might need for use in a particular service. Leaders should seek to become as familiar as possible with the hymnal, in order to be able without too much haphazard searching to find hymns suited to their purpose.

5

Making the Most of Scripture

WE ALREADY HAVE INDICATED the wide possibilities for the use of Scripture with hymns and as calls to worship. We shall now consider the matter of making the Scripture reading, as such, a significant factor in achieving desired worship results. Again we would point out that the deliberate effort to achieve variety without the sacrifice of dignity will prove richly rewarding. The important thing always is to carry out carefully and well the plans made. Novel devices awkwardly or carelessly used offend the sensibilities of people of every age group. The use of the new and unfamiliar will be distracting rather than helpful in achieving the ends of true worship, unless such use is marked by both reverence and some degree of skill.

A CALL TO SCRIPTURE READING

The usual blunt announcement of the Scripture lesson fails to stimulate a spirit of interested expectancy concerning the portion to be read. It is always valuable for the reader to introduce the lesson passage with an arresting bit of poetry concerning the Bible, a Bible verse exalting the Word of God, or a brief statement of one's own—or of some noted writer—as to the merit of the passage to be read.

The hymnbook, any volume of religious poetry, and other sources will furnish suitable poetry regarding the Word of God.

One such passage could be used repeatedly. A group of five or six, used alternately, would serve for many meetings.

Such poems as the following are of the type we recommend here:

> The Bible? That's the Book, the Book indeed,
>> The Book of books
>> On which who looks
> As he should do, aright, shall never need
>> Wish for a better light
>> To guide him in the night.
>>> GEORGE HERBERT

> Thy word is like a garden, Lord,
> With flowers rich and rare;
> And everyone who seeks may pluck
> A lovely cluster there.
>> EDWIN HODDER

> More light shall break from out Thy Word
>> For pilgrim followers of the gleam,
> Till, led by Thy free spirit, Lord,
>> We see and share the Pilgrim dream!
>>> ALLEN CROSS

> We search the world for truth. We cull
> The good, the true, the beautiful,
> From graven stone and written scroll,
> And all old flower-fields of the soul;
> And, weary seekers of the best,
> We come back laden from our quest,
> To find that all the sages said
> Is in the Book our mothers read.
>> JOHN G. WHITTIER

A quotation by a well-known person concerning the Bible will serve as an effective introduction to a Scripture portion.

Think, for example, of the value of thus using such quotations as the following:

In all the ages men have gone to the Bible as to the very springs of thought and inspiration. This book lent Milton his *Paradise Lost;* lent Handel his *The Messiah;* lent Raphael his *Transfiguration;* lent liberty to Cromwell; lent Lincoln a rule "golden" for white and black alike.

NEWELL DWIGHT HILLIS

Yes, it is a homely old book, modest as nature—a book as full of love and blessing as the old mother who reads it with her dear trembling lips—and this book is *the* Book, the Bible. He who has lost his God can find Him again in this Book, and he who has never known Him is here struck with the breath of the Divine Word.

PHILLIPS BROOKS

I speak as a man of the world to men of the world, and I say to you: Search the scriptures. The Bible is the Book of all others to be read at all ages and in all conditions of human life; not to be read once or twice or thrice through, and then laid aside; but to be read in small portions of one or two chapters a day and never to be omitted unless by some overwhelming necessity.

JOHN QUINCY ADAMS

Another great American, Ulysses S. Grant, said, "Hold fast to the Bible as the sheet anchor to your liberties. Write its precepts in your hearts and practice them in your lives."

Dr. David J. Burrell, talking with a seminary student, said, "The Bible is the only authority we have for believing in Christ." The student replied, "Do you mean that Christ and the Bible stand or fall together?" "No," exclaimed Dr. Burrell, "they *stand* together."

Scripture passages are effective in introducing reading. Consider these:

Whosoever heareth these sayings of mine, and doeth them, I will liken him unto a wise man, which built his house upon a rock: and the rain descended, and the floods came, and the winds blew, and beat upon that house; and it fell not: for it was founded upon a rock (Matt. 7:24–25).

For all flesh is as grass, and all the glory of man as the flower of grass. The grass withereth, and the flower thereof falleth away: but the word of the Lord endureth forever. And this is the word which by the gospel is preached unto you (1 Peter 1:24–25).

We have also a more sure word of prophecy; whereunto ye do well that ye take heed, as unto a light that shineth in a dark place, until the day dawn, and the day star arise in your hearts. . . . For the prophecy came not in old time by the will of man: but holy men of God spake as they were moved by the Holy Ghost (2 Peter 1:19, 21).

And many other signs truly did Jesus in the presence of his disciples, which are not written in this book: But these are written that ye might believe that Jesus is the Christ, the Son of God; and that believing ye might have life through his name (John 20:30–31).

The parable of the sower, Mark 4:13–20, may be used in whole or in part as an impressive reminder of the importance for the seed of the Word to fall on good soil.

Introductory statements similar to those just quoted are effective when someone other than the reader uses them. It may be the chairman of the meeting or someone named to render this service. A good voice and clear enunciation are important. In longer passages, such as the last verses of Matthew 7, a choral reading group of four or six, with a blend of heavy and light voices, may be used to recite the call in unison, making sure of uniform timing and clear articulation.

When no such statement from poetry or Scripture is used to

lead into the reading of the Scripture lesson, it is helpful, and advisable, to use a sentence such as the following:

1. "Let us hear the Word of God as it is recorded in the _____ chapter of _____."
2. "Hear the Word of God as revealed to _(name writer)_ and recorded in the _____ chapter of his _____ (book, epistle, or Gospel)."
3. "Let us wait upon God as he speaks to us through the inspired Scriptures."
4. "Let us give heed to the Word of God, dedicating ourselves as we listen to the way of faith and obedience."

At the conclusion of a Scripture reading such words as the following may be used:

1. "May this Word of God abide in your hearts forever."
2. "May God lay this truth upon our hearts, and strengthen us to keep it daily."
3. "To your hearing of this inspired Word may understanding and obedience be added."
4. "Here endeth the reading of the portion of Scripture selected for our hearing today."
5. "May the Spirit of God interpret to you the Word that has been read."

CHORAL READINGS

"Choral readings," as the phrase suggests, refer to the technique of reading by a trained group of people selected for the quality and blend of their voices. Such a group of four or more will have voices of soprano, alto, tenor, and bass quality, broadly speaking, or, more simply, the voices will be *heavy* and *light*. After the group has come to appreciate the passage genuinely as a result of careful instruction concerning the meaning, spirit, and literary quality of the selection to be given, they will memorize it. Then by guided practice a leader will direct them in securing proper rhythm, enunciation, emphasis, and sympathetic interpretation in the reading of the passage.

While all this sounds somewhat technical, it actually is possible for any group of young people or adults to secure fine effects in choral reading. Careful enunciation, increase or decrease of tempo, swelling or diminishing of the sound volume, sectional reading and responses—all these can be employed readily by any leader with a good ear for harmony and a true appreciation of the response desired in an audience to the reading of a passage.

When a well-poised group stands together on a platform and gives an impressive choral reading of a suitable Scripture passage, the audience is always impressed, and their appreciation of the beauty and meaning of the passage greatly enhanced.

Typical passages for use as choral readings are: Isaiah 52: 1–12; Isaiah 55; Ecclesiastes 12; the Beatitudes, Matthew 5:1–11 (given responsively by sections of the choral group); Matthew 7:21–29; Matthew 23:1–12; Matthew 23:13–31; Luke 15: 11–24; John 1:1–14; almost any psalm. These are but a few illustrative selections from among hundreds which, because of their rhythmic quality, beauty of diction, and dramatic effect, would lend themselves to the choral reading technique.

Choral reading selections could be used as processional calls to worship, as prayers, in connection with pantomime, tableau, or pageant, as a prelude or postlude to an anthem, and so on.

Using the Newer Translations

Occasionally the value of a biblical passage is emphasized, and its meaning clarified, when it is read from one of the newer translations, such as Moffatt's, Montgomery's, Goodspeed's, Weymouth's, the English or American Revised Version, and Moulton's. Of these, the more commonly used are the American Revised Version, Moffatt's translation, and Weymouth's translation.

It is both interesting and worth while to have two readers read alternately the same verses of Scripture, first from the Authorized or King James Version, and then from a newer translation. For example, using 1 Corinthians 13, have a reader read the first verse from the King James Version, the second reader then reading it from Weymouth's translation, and so on through the passage. Variety, and even added interest, could be achieved by distributing single verses of the passage in the Moffatt translation among the audience and, as the reader from the Authorized Version reads a verse, the person in the audience holding the same verse in the Moffatt translation reads it as a response. Other versions could be similarly used.

BIBLE MOSAICS

A mosaic is an artistic pattern made up of materials of various colors and shapes, fitted together harmoniously so as to produce beauty and utility.

So a Bible mosaic is a grouping together into a single Scripture reading of passages relating to the worship theme, but taken from various parts of the Bible with aid of a concordance. If the worship theme is "Faith," for example, a Bible mosaic to be read as part of the worship service could be:

Without faith it is impossible to please him (God) (Heb. 11:6). According to your faith be it unto you (Matt. 9:29). This is the victory that overcometh the world, even our faith (1 John 5:4). I am crucified with Christ: nevertheless I live; yet not I, but Christ liveth in me: and the life which I now live in the flesh I live by the faith of the Son of God, who loved me, and gave himself for me (Gal. 2:20).

Abraham believed God, and it was accounted to him for righteousness. Know ye therefore that they which are of faith, the same are the children of Abraham. . . . So then they which be of faith are blessed with faithful Abraham (Gal. 3:6–7, 9). What doth it profit, my brethren, though a man say he hath faith, and have not works? can faith save him? If a brother or sister be naked, and destitute of daily food, And one of you say unto them, Depart in peace, be ye warmed and filled; notwithstanding ye give them not those things which are needful to the body; what doth it profit? Even so faith, if it hath not works, is dead, being alone. Yea, a man may say, Thou hast faith, and I have works: shew me thy faith without thy works, and I will shew thee my faith by my works (James 2:14–18).

Now faith is the substance of things hoped for, the evidence of things not seen (Heb. 11:1). Wherefore seeing we also are compassed about with so great a cloud of witnesses, let us lay aside every weight, and the sin which doth so easily beset us, and let us run with patience the race that is set before us, looking unto Jesus the author and finisher of our faith; who for the joy that was before him endured the cross, despising the shame, and is set down at the right hand of the throne of God (Heb. 12:1–2).

A Scripture mosaic read by one person should be written or typed out on one sheet of paper to make unnecessary a feverish searching for another passage when one has been finished. A series of related passages coming to a climax could be read as a mosaic by a group, each person reading one of the contributing passages. In such cases the passages may be read directly from the Bible since each reader can have his particular passage looked up and ready to read. It is not necessary to announce the Scripture references used, unless desired.

Scripture Used with Religious Art

A Scripture reading will be greatly enriched in interest and value if an attractive reproduction of a masterpiece of religious art portraying the content of a Scripture lesson is used in conjunction with the reading.

Lights are dimmed in the meeting place with a bright light focused on the picture, which is placed on a table near enough to the audience to be seen easily (a lantern slide presentation of the picture would be better still). The reader then presents the passage as the group views the picture reverently.

By way of illustration, the following pictures could be used with the Scripture passages indicated.

Picture	Artist	Related Passage
"Christ and the Doctors"	Hofmann	Luke 2:41–52
"Christ and the Fishermen"	Zimmermann	Mark 1:14–20; Matt. 4:18–20
"Come unto Me"	Bloch	Matt. 11:28–30
"The Lost Sheep"	Soord	Luke 15:1–7
"The Light of the World"	Holman Hunt	John 10:11–16
"Christ with Mary and Martha"	Siemiradzki	Luke 10:38–42
"Christ Entering Jerusalem"	Doré	Luke 19:28–40; Matt. 21:1–9
"Peter's Denial"	Harrach	Luke 22:54–62
"Christ Before Pilate"	Munkácsy	John 18:28–38
"Christ in Gethsemane"	Hofmann	Matt. 26:36–46
"The Entombment"	Ciseri	John 19:34–42
"Holy Women at the Tomb"	Ender	Mark 16:1–8

DRAMA WITH SCRIPTURE READING

Tableau.—A tableau has been described as a "living picture." For our purpose, it is an individual or a group of people (usually the latter) representing without words or action a scene described in the Bible reading. Bible costumes for use in arranging a tableau are easily planned. Properties may be made up largely of towels or scarves for turbans and sashes; and drapes, blankets, shawls, or bathrobes borrowed for costume-making. A chest of such materials should be built up for ready access on the church premises.

As a reader proceeds with the Scripture account of an event, curtains are unobtrusively drawn aside at points in the story decided upon, revealing a tableau portrayal of a high point in the account.

Typical scenes lending themselves to tableau representation are:

> Moses and the Burning Bush (Ex. 3:1–12)
> Moses Returns with the Ten Commandments (Ex. 20)
> "Thou Art the Man" (2 Sam. 12:1–10)
> Water from the Well of Bethlehem (2 Sam. 23:14–17)
> Naboth Refuses to Sell His Vineyard (1 Kings 21:1–4
> Naaman Saved by the Maid of Israel (2 Kings 5:1–14)
> Daniel Prayed as He Had Done Aforetime (Dan. 6:6–10)
> The Good Samaritan (Luke 10)
> The Return of the Prodigal (Luke 15)
> Peter's Denial (John 18:25–27 and parallel passages)
> Saul's Conversion (Acts 9)
> Peter Welcomed by Rhoda (Acts 12:11–17)
> Philip and the Ethiopian Eunuch (Acts 8:26–38)

Scenes involving the appearance of Jesus should, of course, be avoided. However, a group looking adoringly toward him at a point outside the tableau would be permissible.

Pantomime.—Pantomime refers to action without speech. The general use would be similar to that outlined above. Those taking part in the pantomime portray a biblical incident by the use of motions, gestures, postures, but without speech. One short practice would be sufficient preparation.

Generally speaking, tableaux lend themselves to scenes where but little action occurs (Ruth and Naomi in conversation, Elisha witnessing the translation of Elijah, David's lament over Saul and Jonathan, and so on), while the pantomime is used where action can scarcely be dispensed with in conveying the spirit of the event (the good Samaritan, Paul and the Philippian jailer, Moses striking the rock, and so on).

Biblical play or pageant.—Simple dramatic portrayal of a Bible event can be planned originally by almost any group, with simple plot planned and dialogue written. However, a play has limited value as an integral part of a worship service because of the length of time required, the unavoidable activity in connection with production, and the danger of departure from needful simplicity. Only the most skilful, spiritual, and sympathetic leader can be entrusted with the use of this technique for worship purposes.

USING SCRIPTURE TO DIRECT SILENT PRAYER

There is justifiably an increased use in worship services of periods of silent prayer and quiet meditation. People are heeding the words, "Be still, and know that I am God," and find that reverent, silent meditation does make God real and near to the heart.

Sometimes it is well to direct the thoughts of worshipers by reading at intervals, during the period of silence, suitable Scripture passages, brief and meaningful. Such sentences should relate definitely to the theme around which the whole service of worship is built. For example, if the theme is "Consecration," the following passages would be suitable:

"If any man will come after me, let him deny himself, and take up his cross, and follow me" (Matt. 16:24). (A pause follows for meditation.)

"If ye then be risen with Christ, seek those things which are above, where Christ sitteth on the right hand of God" (Col. 3:1).

"That ye may be sincere and without offence till the day of Christ; Being filled with the fruits of righteousness, which are by Jesus Christ, unto the glory and praise of God" (Phil. 1:10–11).

It should be noted here that many hymn stanzas, or portions of stanzas, are valuable for use in directing the thought of silent worshipers.

DESCRIPTIVE INTRODUCTION TO SCRIPTURE LESSON

When a Scripture reading refers to events centering in a specific place, it is valuable to precede or follow the Scripture lesson with a short descriptive reading about the place concerned. Such cities or towns as Jericho, Samaria, Philippi, Ephesus, and many others, are beautifully described in H. C. V. Morton's books, *In the Steps of the Master, In the Steps of St. Paul,* and *Through Lands of the Bible.* A paragraph or two from one of these books read before or after a Scripture lesson would add much to the appreciation of the lesson. Any Bible commentary would also furnish useful materials of this type.

The foregoing suggestions are indicative of the possibilities of varied uses of Scripture without any sacrifice of befitting dignity and motive. A little inspired thinking plus a bit of diligent searching in likely places are the chief conditions to be met by those who would create worship services that will honor God and lift up the hearts of his people.

6

Prayer, the Soul of Worship

PRAYER IS THE SOUL of worship. It is the mind questing for truth, the heart longing for peace, the spirit thirsting for fuller life. It is the mystic, sure way to the throne of grace. It is the soul's converse with its Maker. It is the divine provision whereby man can communicate with God. It is release from time into eternity, from the temporal into the spiritual, from the life of the flesh to the realm of the spirit. It is the realm of reality where man recognizes himself as properly and inescapably a creature of two worlds—"the world that now is, and the world that is to come." No one has put it more exactly or beautifully than James Montgomery, who wrote in 1818 these haunting words:

> Prayer is the soul's sincere desire,
>   Uttered or unexpressed;
> The motion of a hidden fire,
>   That trembles in the breast.
>
> Prayer is the Christian's vital breath,
>   The Christian's native air;
> His watchword at the gates of death—
>   He enters heaven with prayer.

And then, realizing that the secret of the purest and most powerful prayer is with the Son of God, the poet goes on to put in poetic form the eager petition of the disciples as they cried, "Lord, teach us to pray." Montgomery concludes his beloved hymn:

> O Thou by whom we come to God—
> The Life, the Truth, the Way!
> The path of prayer Thyself hast trod;
> Lord, teach us how to pray!

Granting, then, the vital place of prayer in the truest worship of Almighty God, it becomes necessary for us to plan with reverent care for the prayer aspects of our worship services. Prayer can be both informal and formal, both spontaneous and planned, both vocal and silent. In no experience of true worship must the spirit be more unfettered than here. In no part of a worship service must there be a more earnest effort to avoid any appearance of dead formalism, perfunctory language, dull repetition, coldness of heart or word. Varied forms of prayer are possible, without any sacrifice of sincerity or feeling. Let us give some thought to those which can be used readily, but with a spirit of reality, by any careful worship leader.

CALLS TO PRAYER

Often prayer is announced somewhat too abruptly. Careful use of calls to prayer helps to induce the spirit of privilege and expectancy which the experience of prayer should suggest. A Scripture passage, a prayer-hymn stanza or stanzas, a moving statement about prayer, a sentence summoning the worshipers to the attitude of mind and heart which prayer requires—all such practices will provide rich returns to those who use them reverently. We do not deny the value of such commonly used sentences as: "Let us all pray"; "Will you all join with me in the spirit of prayer"; "Let us all share in the privilege of prayer."

We simply stress the fact that, in keeping with the thesis of this volume, there is a vitality in variety carefully used. Nothing should be used in calling others to prayer which cannot be used naturally, quietly, reverently.

Scripture Calls to Prayer

A Scripture call to prayer can be given just after the leader has said, "Let us pray," or "Let us approach God in prayer," or other sentences of the kind, as mentioned before. Or, as a variant, the Scripture call can be given first, followed by "Let us, therefore, pray, for God has invited us to come." Some helpful Scripture calls to prayer follow (the reference is not read):

For the Lord will not forsake his people for his great name's sake: because it hath pleased the Lord to make you his people. . . . God forbid that I should sin against the Lord in ceasing to pray for you (1 Sam. 12:22–23).

If my people, which are called by my name, shall humble themselves, and pray, and seek my face, and turn from their wicked ways; then will I hear from heaven, and will forgive their sin, and will heal their land (2 Chron. 7:14).

Give ear to my words, O Lord, consider my meditation. Hearken unto the voice of my cry, my King, and my God: for unto thee will I pray (Psalm 5:1–2).

Praise waiteth for thee, O God, in Sion: and unto thee shall the vow be performed: O thou that hearest prayer, unto thee shall all flesh come (Psalm 65:1–2).

Ask, and it shall be given you; seek, and ye shall find; knock, and it shall be opened unto you: For every one that asketh receiveth; and he that seeketh findeth; and to him that knocketh it shall be opened (Matt. 7:7–8).

If ye have faith as a grain of mustard seed, ye shall say unto this mountain, Remove hence to yonder place . . . and nothing shall be impossible unto you. Howbeit this kind goeth not out but by prayer and fasting (Matt. 17:20–21).

Watch ye and pray, lest ye enter into temptation. The spirit truly is ready, but the flesh is weak (Mark 14:38).

The book of Psalms abounds in such passages; see 6:9; 66:19–20; 88:1–2; 141:1–2. See also Mark 11:22–26; Luke 11:1; 1 Thessalonians 5:16–18; Ephesians 6:18; 1 Peter 3:12.

A concordance will provide many more Scripture calls under the words "pray," "prayer," "prayed." If a brief one is used, such as "Pray without ceasing," it sounds abrupt. In such a case precede it with this type of sentence: "Let us remember the words of the apostle Paul, how he counseled the Christians of Thessalonica with these words. . . ."

Hymnal Calls to Prayer

There are many hymns which, in whole or in part, serve as effective calls to prayer. It is well for a person to own his own hymnbook and index some of its worship material for himself on blank pages at the back of it. The best way to accomplish this is to list hymn and hymn stanza references in the back of the hymnary as they come to your notice—during the singing of a hymn, as you read in the hymnbook prior to the opening of a service, as you have a hymn-sing at home. If you are singing the hymn "Just as I Am," you might well say to yourself, "What an effective call to prayer, or to worship, that stanza would be." At that point list the hymn number in the back of your hymnbook under the heading "Calls to Worship" or "Calls to Prayer."

Varied uses of hymns as calls to prayer are possible. For instance, let us seek to use one stanza of the favorite hymn

"What a Friend We Have in Jesus" in a somewhat unusual way. A choir might be divided into two groups, each to sing a line of the hymn alternately. Or, one group could sing the first four lines, and the other the remaining four lines.

GROUP 1: "What a friend we have in Jesus,"
GROUP 2: "All our sins and griefs to bear!"
GROUP 1: "What a privilege to carry"
GROUP 2: "Everything to God in prayer!"
GROUP 1: "Oh, what peace we often forfeit,"
GROUP 2: "Oh, what needless pain we bear,"
GROUP 1: "All because we do not carry"
GROUP 2: "Everything to God in prayer!"

A variation would include meditation for a few seconds on a picture of Jesus which has been placed on an easel before the group (spotlight or strong flashlight turned on it). Then two lines of the stanza are sung in turn by each of four singers throughout the group, without piano accompaniment or with it, as preferred. A hymnbook should not be required for such a familiar stanza, and it would be effective to have very dim lights, with the exception of the bright light focused on the picture.

It would be effective also if, following this quiet singing, the group remains bowed in prayer for a few seconds longer, while the piano or organ plays the stanza through again softly, following which the leader says "Amen."

Any worship leader can find numerous hymns which, in whole or in part, can be used to advantage as calls to prayers. Usually one stanza is sufficient. The following list is but suggestive of the type to be selected.

"Approach, My Soul, the Mercy-Seat"
"Come, Ye Disconsolate"
"From Every Stormy Wind That Blows"

"Lord, I Hear of Showers of Blessings"
" 'Tis the Blessed Hour of Prayer"
"Whisper a Prayer in the Morning" (and many choruses
  of good quality)

Such hymns can be used in many ways: as solos; sung by the
whole group, or by two groups antiphonally; read in unison, or
by the leader; used (as mentioned) in connection with a suitable picture; sung by a duet, trio, or quartet.

Poems as Calls to Prayer

Many poems, now used for hymn purposes, are equally valuable as calls to prayer. They are deeply devotional and help
to fix the thoughts of the worshipers upon the true objectives
of worship. The volumes of poems mentioned at other points
in this book contain many poems which are, in spirit, calls to
prayer. Used by themselves, or in conjunction with Scripture,
hymns, and pictures, they can be valuable to the spirit and
power of services of worship. A few sample poems follow,
selected from James Dalton Morrison's anthology *Masterpieces
of Religious Verse*.

> O world, thou choosest not the better part!
> It is not wisdom to be only wise,
> And on the inward vision close the eyes;
>
> .   .   .   .
> Our knowledge is a torch of smoky pine
> That lights the pathway but one step ahead
> Across a void of mystery and dread.
> Bid, then, the tender light of faith to shine
> By which alone the mortal heart is led
> Unto the thinking of the thought divine.
>
> GEORGE SANTAYANA

> Better a day of faith
> Than a thousand years of doubt!

63

Better one mortal hour with Thee
Than an endless life without!

Thou art a mighty Wall,
Skirting life's darkened stair;
Groping my way alone,
Lo, I have found Thee there!
HENRY BURKE ROBINS

So through the clouds of Calvary—there shines
His face, and I believe that Evil dies,
And Good lives on, loves on, and conquers all—
All War must end in Peace. These clouds are lies.
They cannot last. The blue sky is the Truth.
For God is Love. Such is my Faith, and such
My reasons for it, and I find them strong
Enough. And you? You want to argue? Well,
I can't. It is a choice. I choose the Christ.
G. A. STUDDERT-KENNEDY

We may not climb the heavenly steeps
To bring the Lord Christ down:
In vain we search the lowest deeps,
For Him no depths can drown.

But warm, sweet, tender, even yet
A present help is He;
And faith has still its Olivet,
And love its Galilee.

. . . .
O Lord and Master of us all!
Whate'er our name or sign,
We own Thy sway, we hear Thy call,
We test our lives by Thine.
JOHN GREENLEAF WHITTIER

Note: In the above poem a selection of three stanzas was made
from a total of seven in the volume. Such selection, serving the

immediate purpose of worship, is often necessary both in the interests of brevity and of appropriateness for the purpose.

> Unworthy? Yes, unworthy.
>   What doest thou here?
> Love's arms are wide to welcome
>   And bring me near.
>
> Unworthy? Yes, unworthy,
>   How dare to pray?
> The Holy Place is open—
>   Love made a way.
>
> Unworthy? Yes, unworthy.
>   How hope for heaven?
> Hope for the poorest sinner
>   By Love is given.
>
> Unworthy? Yes, unworthy.
>   Hast thou no fear?
> Fear fleeth love's pure presence,
>   And love is here.
>
> E. MARGARET CLARKSON

Poems used as calls to prayer should dwell on such themes as the love of God, man's faith in God, the nature of prayer itself. Those chosen should not be too long. They should be read distinctly and with feeling and good expression. When they can be memorized and recited, their effect is increased. It would be helpful to file away carefully any poems which might be of value for future use.

GREAT BIBLE PRAYERS

There is a goodly number of great prayers to be found in the Bible itself. It is exceedingly worth while to use one of these occasionally, when they fit the theme in hand. Some great

Bible prayers are: Moses' prayer, Exodus 33:12–13; Hannah's prayer, 1 Samuel 2:1 ff.; Solomon's prayer at the dedication of the Temple, 1 Kings 8:22–53; Hezekiah's prayer, 2 Kings 19:15–19; Nehemiah's prayer, Nehemiah 1:5–11; Daniel's prayer, Daniel 9; the prayer in Habakkuk 3. There are many in the Psalms, of course, to be found readily.

Prayer Hymns

Many of the best-loved hymns are prayers in themselves, and should be sung and otherwise used as such. They can be sung by the group, sung in solo fashion, read in unison by the group, by the leader, or by a small group as a choral reading. Used thoughtfully and with care, they can add much to the spirit and power of a prayer period. We list here, only by way of illustrating the wide selection available, a few of the well-known prayer hymns.

"Lord, Teach Us How to Pray Aright"
"Spirit Divine, Attend Our Prayers"
"Prayer Is the Soul's Sincere Desire"
"My God, Is Any Hour So Sweet"
"Lord of Our Life, and God of Our Salvation"
"Dear Lord and Father of Mankind"
"Spirit of God, Descend upon My Heart"
"Jesus, Thou Joy of Loving Hearts"
"Lord, for Tomorrow and Its Needs"
"Whiter Than Snow"

Prepared Prayers

While we would deplore any trend toward the reading of written or printed prayers as a habit, much can be said as to the value of the occasional well-planned use of great prayers prepared by masters of the high art of prayerful expression. The occasional use of such prayers helps to establish a standard of devotional language which can enrich the prayer life of the individual and of the congregation over a period of time. Too much dependence on well-worn phrases and repetitious sentences is to be avoided, and the use of classic printed prayers will help in this. It becomes easy, however, to lean too much on this kind of prayer. After all, the most effectual prayer is spontaneous, proceeding from the individual's own heart of love for Christ, related to his own sense of need, and vitalized by his own faith.

Many volumes of prayer are available in bookstores. *God's Minute* has a short prayer for each day of a whole year. *Open the Meeting with Prayer* is a useful collection published by the Concordia Publishing House. Dr. John Baillie's *A Diary of Private Prayer* (Scribner's Sons) is one to own without fail. *Prayers for All Occasions,* by Stuart R. Oglesby, is very useful.

The Use of Group or Corporate Prayers

The participation of the entire group in audible prayer can be an effective part of a worshipful experience. It has the value of enabling the shy, backward, and inexperienced person in the group to pray aloud, thus becoming accustomed to the sound of his own voice in intercession and experiencing the uplift of being an active unit in a prayer group.

It has been said that worthy and effective intercession involves three elements: (1) a sincere desire for the highest good of the person or cause for which prayer is offered; (2) utmost confidence in God's readiness and sufficiency to answer prayer; (3) an obedient readiness to become an instrument in God's hand as he provides an answer to our prayers (see Matt. 9:35 to 10:15). Effort is required on the part of the worship leader to lead all to a proper appreciation of the privilege and responsibility of prayer, and a surrender to the spirit through which prayer becomes acceptable to God and sanctifying to man.

Group praying may be in the form of any of the following:
1. A prayer hymn—either read in unison, or sung as a group.
2. A prayer poem in unison—from mimeographed copies in hand, or from a slide or crayon copy displayed before the group.
3. A unison prayer—from the hymnary, the Bible, a mimeographed copy, or a slide.

The most common, and perhaps the most effective, form of unison prayer is the *litany*. The litany is a responsive prayer in which the leader offers a petition of one or two sentences, following which the group replies with a brief response in which its members have been instructed carefully prior to the prayer period. The litany should have a unifying theme and should progress to a climax.

The following litany illustrates the nature and value of this prayer device. The response to each brief petition of the leader will be, "Hear our thanksgiving, O Lord," or "We give thee thanks, O Lord." The leader's "Amen" will end the prayer. (Such instructions must be given briefly, but clearly, just before the litany of prayer begins.)

Thanksgiving

LEADER: Eternal God, giver of every good and perfect gift, for thine infinite love made known to men in creation and in the wondrous plan of salvation in thy Son, Jesus Christ our Lord,

GROUP: Hear our thanksgiving, O Lord.

LEADER: For the beauty and fertility of the earth, providing food for the body and soul of thy children,

GROUP: Hear our thanksgiving, O Lord.

LEADER: For the sure succession of the seasons, with their infinite variety of wonder and beauty, and with their constant witness to thy power and providence,

GROUP: Hear our thanksgiving, O Lord.

LEADER: For thy love for sinful, weak, and erring humanity, and for the gracious provision of a Saviour through whom we can, by faith, become more than conquerors over sin and death,

GROUP: Hear our thanksgiving, O Lord.

LEADER: For the ever present help and guidance of thy Holy Spirit, through whom we overcome temptation, discover and follow the way of eternal life, behold and ever seek after the City of God,

GROUP: Hear our thanksgiving, O Lord.

LEADER: Let us conclude our prayer by uniting in the words of the Lord's Prayer.

The Church

LEADER: Eternal God, by whose infinite grace Jesus Christ became the head and cornerstone of the church, and for which he gave his own precious blood, let thy richest blessing rest upon thy people in all the earth in this hour of the world's need.

GROUP: Hear our prayer, O Lord, and answer us.

LEADER: Grant unto all ministers of the gospel the spirit of understanding and love, the courage to declare the truth even when it is not welcomed because of human sinfulness, the loving heart from which proceedeth patience, understanding, and compassionate service.

GROUP: Hear our prayer, O Lord, and answer us.

LEADER: Guide the labors of all who teach the young in Thy name, that they may know Thy love in their own hearts, study Thy truth with diligence, lead the young with tenderness and grace, and bring them to the hour of decision wherein they shall accept Thee as Saviour and Lord, as Redeemer and Friend.

GROUP: Hear our prayer, O Lord, and answer us.

LEADER: Be pleased to draw near to all who serve Thy cause in faraway places of the earth. Fortify them in every hour of trial; encourage them when seed faithfully sown seems to fall on barren soil; help them to find in Thee, day by day, all needed resources of wisdom, faith, endurance, and conviction.

GROUP: Hear our prayer, O Lord, and answer us.

LEADER: Bless us all, O Lord, that we may faithfully perform our sacred vows from day to day and in all circumstances, imparting to thy church increasing influence and attractiveness because of the faithfulness of our witness, and the worthiness with which we manifest thy spirit in all our decisions, deeds, and words.

GROUP: Hear our prayer, O Lord, and answer us.

LEADER: Amen.

Litanies should be thought out and written down ahead of time. Often they are mimeographed, so that every member of the group has one. Where an order of service is used, the litany would naturally appear there. If copies are not in every hand, careful instruction in the group response is needed. Other aids in this respect are to write the response on a blackboard, or in black crayon on a large sheet of paper on the wall or an easel. A simpler, and, in some respects, better plan is to have four or five people in the group furnished with carbon typewritten copies of the whole litany, so that they may lead in the responses at the exact moments. Others readily can follow such leads.

The litany should not be too long and should have a central theme. As a general rule, avoid more than six or eight petitions and responses. Occasionally, the leader's petitions may be entirely in the form of passages of Scripture, to which the response might be: "Help us to obey this Thy word."

The *bidding prayer,* or *directed silent prayer,* as it is more commonly called, is of value also. Here the leader offers a petition to guide the prayerful spirit of the group. At the end of each short petition, the leader pauses, saying, "Let us all pray to this end," or "Let each of us, in silent prayer, beseech God's answer to this prayer." The exact response will vary according to the nature of the prayer—petition, confession, thanksgiving, adoration.

Such a bidding prayer might use the words of a portion of Scripture. For example, 1 Corinthians 13 might be used. As each unit of thought in the passage is read, the leader pauses and says, "Let us pray for this grace in our own hearts." The Beatitudes could be used in the same way. So also could Psalm 1 and a host of passages besides.

Ordinarily, however, the leader offers a prayer which divides naturally into sections, asking after each for the group to join him silently in seeking God's response to the petition. A very short bidding prayer follows, to illustrate the form. The theme of the prayer is "Discipleship."

Eternal God, who hast not left thyself without witness in any generation, and who delightest to honor the sons of men with places of service and responsibility in the tasks of thy kingdom, grant, we pray thee, that all of us in thy presence here may hear thy call to serve in thy vineyard, and may dedicate ourselves in all sincerity, and with abounding joy, to the doing of thy will in the world. Let us pray. (*A silence of ten seconds follows these words each time.*)

Grant that we may be true and constant witnesses to thy grace and truth before men, encouraging the weak, guiding the erring, comforting those who mourn, restraining the reckless, offering thy merciful redemption to those who have sinned and who long for purity and power. Let us pray. . . .

Give us a full portion, day by day, of the joy of thy salvation—the joy of knowing that our sins have been forgiven, that we have received through Christ the spirit of adoption whereby we may call thee Father, that thy strength is perfected in our weakness, and that neither life nor death can separate from thine unfailing and unfathomable love. Let us pray. . . .

Be pleased to bring us into increasing spiritual maturity, to the fulness of the stature that is in Christ Jesus our Lord. To this end help us to grow in wisdom and in understanding, in patience and in tolerance, in insight and compassion, in unselfishness and thoughtfulness, in self-control and the spirit of sacrifice. Let us pray. . . . (*After the period of silence, the leader concludes the prayer with "Amen."*)

Some leaders like soft music—piano, organ, violin—during the periods of silence, with the music of a well-known hymn of intercession used, such as "Breathe on Me, Breath of God," "When I Survey the Wondrous Cross," "Take Time to Be Holy," and others. Occasionally a small group in the meeting may hum softly as the others engage in silent prayer. These practices must be determined by the sensitivity of the leader, and by the capacity of the group to co-operate understandingly in all that the leader asks for.

Many books of worship services will contain litanies, but the dicipline of preparing them ourselves is a rich one. The more exact appropriateness of prayers provided for our people—with their particular needs, problems, aspirations, opportunities, and challenges—makes them much to be preferred to ready-made prayers, though, as we have said, there is rich value in the occasional use of ready-made prayers, provided they are used with reverence and with the resolve to make them our own as we offer them.

Let us repeat our emphasis on the need for the leader of

group prayer to be well prepared and in the spirit of prayer. The call to prayer must be unhurried, earnest, and expressed in strong words from the Scriptures (see the section on "Calls to Prayer" in a previous chapter). The responses used with litanies must be well phrased, and must vary according to the theme. It may be helpful to suggest here a few additional Scripture passages relating to prayer, which may be used in relation to the above exhortation.

1. The way of prayer: Luke 11:1–4; 18:1–14; Mark 11:25; Hebrews 11:6.

2. Sincerity in prayer: Matthew 6:5–8; 11:25–30; Mark 11:22–26.

3. Prayer as service to God: Isaiah 50:4; Matthew 10:40–42; 25:31–40; Luke 10:25–27.

4. Prayers are heard: Isaiah 55:6–11; Psalm 20; John 16:23–28; Acts 2:1–4.

We have dealt with directed silent prayer by an entire group. But there is a place for fully silent prayer. So often our greatest need is to rest awhile in the empowering stillness which means communion with God. A leader may call the group to silent prayer with such introductions as the following: (1) a hymn of meditation sung as a solo; (2) a devotional poem (often on prayer itself); (3) the announcement of some urgent need for prayer in the church family, or an earnest request from a missionary's letter; (4) a brief introductory prayer by the leader, followed by silent prayer by all; (5) a moving passage of Scripture which stirs the mind and heart of the hearers to prayerful petition for forgiveness, dedication, obedience.

PRAYERS OFFERED BY INDIVIDUALS

With all the undoubted values deriving from the use of various types of group prayer, it remains ever true that "the effectual fervent prayer of a righteous man availeth much."

The perennial danger to be avoided in prayers offered by individuals, either voluntarily or in response to a call from the leader, is "much speaking, and vain repetition." These faults can be avoided only by thoughtful preparation, the most effective of which must ever be the disciplining of oneself in private devotions at home. If in a person's daily devotions specific objects of prayer are selected and beauty of expression is sought, it follows that prayer offered in public will influence others to pray.

While prayer should not be confined to the limits of any fixed formula, it is helpful to know that there is a somewhat accepted structure for worthy prayer. The writer has been grateful for the outline supplied by the acrostic on the word "Acts" (referred to in chap. 2). To follow some such progression of thought as this will give clarity and order to a public prayer. "Praise, penitence, and petition" (praise to include thanksgiving) is another simple formula which redeems many a prayer from aimlessness. Extemporaneous prayer can be very rambling and incoherent unless some general guide is known to the one who is asked to pray.

In concluding this section on prayer, we repeat that the vital success of a worship service will depend largely upon the genuineness and power of the group's prayer experience. We need to pray often and earnestly, "Lord, teach us to pray: for we know not what to pray for as we ought."

7

Stories, Biography, and Quotations

A CHINESE PROVERB DECLARES, "One picture speaks ten thousand words." We might paraphrase this ancient statement by saying, "One word picture in the form of a good story or a fine quotation speaks ten thousand words of inspiration." Jesus made ample use of this teaching technique. Such material should be well presented and to the point, if its worship value is to be emphasized.

A worship notebook of helps like these and others already discussed might be kept.

STORIES

Stories are of timeless interest and value for leaders of worship. They have the merit and distinction of being equally valuable for the young and the old, for youth and busy middle age. The frequent use of parables by our Lord gives supreme authority for the presentation of truth in story form. There are innumerable sources of stories; the supply is unending. All that is needed by an alert worship leader is a simple system for recording stories discovered, and good judgment in relating them to themes and occasions when they can be used with maximum effect in relation to a high purpose.

In well-planned worship services stories can be used in any of the following ways:

1. In place of a devotional talk or meditation on the worship theme.
2. To illustrate the meaning of a passage of Scripture used.
3. To give particular point to the offering, and motivation therefor.
4. To lead up to a period of prayer (as, for instance, in using a missionary story).
5. To prepare the group for the worship experience itself.
6. To provide an incident to be dramatized in some such form as: dialogue; simple play; pantomime; tableaux accompanying the telling of the story; film or slides.
7. To interpret or emphasize the meaning of a solo, choral number, or hymn which is to follow, or be followed.

As we have said, there are almost unlimited sources of brief stories to be used for worship services of vital meaning. We shall mention some of these very accessible sources and use one or more stories of the type which each source should supply.

Bible Stories

One good book is a better investment—at any price—than a dozen poor ones! However, the stories appearing in the Bible itself are fascinating, and, told in his own language by one who loves the Word of God, can be very gripping. Christian leaders should not depend entirely on "ready-to-use" Bible stories. They should master the content of stories themselves, and then share them in warm, vivid language with their people. Consider how effectively such stories as the following could be used direct from the scriptural record: Gideon's call and adventures (Judg. 6–7); the story of two brothers, Abraham and Lot (Gen. 13); the stirring story of Naboth and his vineyard (1 Kings 21); Jeremiah rescued by Ebed-melech (Jer. 38); Daniel's defiance of an evil decree (Dan. 6); Philip and the Ethiopian eunuch (Acts 8). These are but illustrations of the variety and number of Bible stories which await your use.

Such well-used books as the following illustrate what is available:

> *Forty Stories for the Church, School and Home* by Margaret W. Eggleston (Harper & Brothers)
> *Glad Days in Galilee* (revised; now *Boy of Nazareth*) by Marian Keith (Abingdon)
> *World Over Stories* by F. W. Lambertson (Abingdon)
> *Stories of the Prophets as Told to Their Friends* by R. Barclay Moon (Cokesbury)
> *Famous Bible Pictures and Stories They Tell* by Elizabeth Bonsall (Union Press)
> *The Red Stocking, and Other Christmas Stories* by Margaret W. Eggleston (Harper & Brothers)

Books

The boundless realm of literature can supply endless numbers of short stories or incidents for fruitful use in worship services. Magazines, novels, classic literature (such as that of Bunyan, Shakespeare, Dickens, Hawthorne, and a host besides), Sunday school papers and lesson helps will all provide material worth filing and using as occasion arises. An example will make this clear.

The following story theme is a powerful attack upon class and national prejudice. It is a story in blank verse, written during World War II by Alice Duer Miller. It is related here in a free conversational way such as would make it effective in a typical worship service.

During World War II a young British officer of blue blood ancestry came home to his mother's country mansion one day

77

and announced that he was going to marry an American nurse. The haughty dowager mother gasped in horror. She loathed Americans. She regarded them as coarse money-grabbers, a nation of grocerymen, and all that. If she had been able to do so, she would have enjoyed telling America by wireless how much she disliked an upstart nation that had the audacity and bad taste to rebel against Britain! Thus her son's announcement shocked and angered her. What had she done to deserve this disgrace!

But love has a way of leaping over ancient grudges and senseless prejudices. The dashing young British officer and the brave American nurse were married. Almost immediately he was posted to the Continent. He said to his bride one day, in effect, "Darling, I have a hard request to make of you. I want you to promise me that on some of your leaves you will go visit mother." Though realizing what this could well mean, the bride agreed. Her husband could face the German tanks all right; surely she could face a mother-in-law at his request!

These visits were a test of her fidelity to a noble vow. Her mother-in-law with ingenious cruelty determined to make this intruder so sorry for her bargain that she would pack up and go back to New York and stay there where she belonged. She insulted the girl, ignored her, misrepresented her to her own friends.

But there was one thing about this girl which she did not know—she was a Christian! And she was the kind of Christian who believed that her faith would work in any situation, however difficult. She also knew that the Christian's secret weapon is patient love. So she met the mother-in-law's insults with silence, her injustice with unselfish labor for her persecutor's comfort, her neglect with thoughtful generosity. And it worked —as it always does, soon or late! Gradually the icy heart of the mother-in-law melted under the steady warmth of the nurse's kindly love. Then one day it happened. She was visiting an old neighbor of many years' standing, and, suddenly, in the midst of a conversation about nothing in particular, John's mother said, "You know, I like Americans; my daughter-in-law is an American."

No more splendid victory can come to a follower of Christ than to conquer in his Spirit, and to bear witness to his Lordship over all of life. We must be his followers not only in word, but in *deed*.

To follow such a story with silent prayer, then with such a hymn as "In Christ There Is No East or West," will move any group to the worship of the God of love, and to purifying resolves to manifest his spirit in life's relationships. After all, worship ought to result in such transforming commitments in a harsh world.

Novels like Thomas Savage's *A Bargain with God* and Lloyd C. Douglas' *The Robe* are full of incidents which can be used with power in services of worship. Another book of similar subject matter is *The Word Lives On*, an anthology edited by Frances Brentano. It is only necessary that the leader be alert to discover and conserve for future use such stories as elevate the thought, stir the heart, humble and challenge the spirit.

Magazines

Frequently a magazine article, biographical sketch, or story will contain a passage which relates to a theme often used in worship services. Consider, for example, the theme of evangelism. In the *Saturday Evening Post* of November 26, 1955, there was an article by Paul Schubert entitled "The Pastor of Bighorn Basin." Speaking of the pastor, whose name is Ray, the writer says:

In fact, Ray's title, "Sunday-school missionary," is a 1955 misnomer. What he does is bring church, not "salvation," to the Wyoming back country. The prosperous, educated and informed people there would be amused and indignant at the very suggestion that they need "conversion," but they are profoundly grateful to the minister who comes to them to conduct regular worship, even once a month.

To read such a statement and follow it with Scripture reading emphasizing all men's need of salvation by faith through the grace of God in Christ Jesus (for example, 1 John 1:8 to 2:2) would be very arresting. To follow this with one or two quiet testimonies and prayer would lead the thought of all worshipers to the foot of the cross of the atonement.

Newspapers

Likewise newspapers frequently contain statements which might be used effectively by worship leaders to stimulate interest, focus attention upon the world's need of a Saviour, remind the worshipers of the activity of God in our time. Reports of crime and social chaos, statistics concerning the dope and liquor traffics, facts about divorce and juvenile delinquency, statements from addresses or reports by statesmen and other notable figures attracting newspaper attention, news about Christian causes at home and abroad, stories of heroism and unselfish acts—these and many themes besides receive newspaper treatment from time to time and furnish quotable material, or data, to be referred to in worship meditations, or prayer themes for periods of silence.

A "newspaper clipping" file will receive weekly contributions, we predict, and will offer valuable aid to the busy leader or those whom he desires to help. Its up-to-dateness will prove a valuable resource to all concerned.

The brief news story which follows concerns a tragic train wreck in the Canadian Rockies.

An official of the Canadian National Railways states that the omission of three words from a train order was responsible for yesterday's collision between a troop train and a transcontinental flier in which sixteen people were killed, with two still missing. The official said that the words "at Canoe River" were dropped from the message given to the conductor of the troop train. The full order should have read something like this: "The troop train will wait *at Canoe River* for Transcontinental Train Number 2 to pass. The troop train will then proceed west to Gosnell, where it will wait for the second section of the Transcontinental Train, Train Number 4, to pass."

With the words "at Canoe River" left out, the troop train got the impression that it was to wait for the *first* section at Gosnell, ten miles west of Canoe River. A few minutes after it passed Canoe River the tragic and costly collision occurred.

How important those three little words were. And, for every man and woman how tremendously important such three little words as "Believe in Me," or "Accept Jesus Christ." To omit those three little words from one's life leads to tragedy and death, too.

The use made of such an incident will vary according to the purpose of the worship leader, but, certainly, such an incident from the daily paper can serve a valuable end.

Queen Elizabeth II of the British Commonwealth broadcast a New Year's message from Buckingham Palace in 1954. The following excerpt from it appeared in the daily papers a day later:

It does indeed seem to me that if the years to come are to see some real spiritual recovery, the women of our nation must be deeply concerned with religion, and our homes are the very places where it should start. It is the creative and dynamic power of Christianity which can help us to carry the moral responsibility which history is placing upon our shoulders. If our homes can be truly Christian, then the influence of that spirit will assuredly spread through all the aspects of our common life, social and political.

Such a quotation would be helpful in a service on the theme of "Home." In a youth group it would be interesting and effective, for example, to have one young person hold a large picture of Queen Elizabeth before the group as the quotation is read, much as television broadcasters often quote eminent people as pictures of the same appear on the television screen.

These two items should serve to indicate the variety and interest of data appearing in the daily press for those gathering material for use in vital worship services.

Travel

Everybody travels today—by train and plane, by car and ship. Surely our "one world" has shrunk into a neighborhood. In travel people who cultivate the art of noticing matters of significance can gather many facts, quotations, and stories to use as Christian leaders. Such items are of value since they are first-person matters which can be both told and heard with particular interest and warmth. The following two incidents from the writer's travels illustrate this thesis.

Not long ago I was traveling by air from New York to Toronto, Canada, on a two-motored American Airlines plane. Midway over New York State a sudden and violent storm roared out of the southwest. Great banks of threatening clouds rolled in; gales of wind swept the port side of the plane. The craft staggered and plunged alarmingly in the blackness of the night. From where I sat I looked out somewhat uneasily, I confess, and could see the port propeller whirling at twenty-five hundred revolutions per minute. In the ray of light from the pilot's control room the propeller looked like a circle of light.

Suddenly I thought how much like a halo it looked. Then I realized that, so long as the propellers were doing their work, we were probably safe. That is to say, *so long as the halo was there* we were all right!

Then I reflected upon life itself. I realized that the halo represents the "holy" in our lives—the spiritual aspects of our nature. I realized also that the "halo" might be applied to our national life—the spiritual aspect of it. And my thoughts went something like this: "Our security, as individuals and as a nation, is found in the strength and reality and power of our spiritual life. If men or nations become purely materialistic and self-centered, spurning the spiritual facts of existence, then they are doomed. They cannot make port. They will crash on the mountain of divine reality. Our security is in recognizing that 'this is the Father's world,' and that 'by grace we are saved through faith.' "

The Christian church and its gospel must keep the "halo" bright in men's lives.

The applications of the story are many. It could be told with the room darkened and with a slide of a stormy sky on the screen. It could be followed by some such hymn as "Jesus, Saviour, Pilot Me," or "Will Your Anchor Hold in the Storms of Life?"

When I was sixteen years of age I went to western Canada to teach school—a distance of three thousand miles from my Nova Scotia home. Not long after my arrival I was invited to go by car with a man whom I scarcely knew to a "stampede" in the Battle River Valley. I had heard about stampedes, with chuck wagon races, steer roping, bucking horse riding, and all the rest, and, at my age, was thrilled to go.

We arrived in the Valley where about two thousand tents were pitched for the week end. Just as we got our tent set up and our supplies carried into it from the car, two men appeared, strangers to me. They proposed that we all go for a walk. After a long trip over dirt roads in a "Model-T" we were glad to stretch our legs.

We walked about a hundred yards to a spot where a dip in the ground appeared behind a screen of poplar bush. There, to my surprise, the men promptly sat down. A bottle of liquor suddenly appeared as from nowhere (those were prohibition days!). After two men had drunk from the bottle it reached me. I knew I was "on the spot." Quietly I said, "No, thanks."

Then the three "went to work on me." In turn they said such things as these: "Come on now, kid; if you're going to live in this man's country, you've got to act like a man." "Remember, you're not tied to your mother's apron strings now." So it went, and I knew I was faced by a decision. I knew, too, that it was to be one of the most important decisions of my life. As I sat there, confused, and alone, I suddenly had a vision. I saw myself six months before going down into the baptistry of a little village church to declare my faith in Christ by baptism. I saw two hundred faces in the congregation—the faces of people who had voted to receive me into the membership of that old church after baptism, people who believed in me, who trusted me to be faithful.

Quickly I realized that I had to choose whom I wished most to please—these three strangers of undisciplined life, or those two hundred friends of Christ's family. I knew which it was to be. Quickly I turned to the men and said quietly, "Gentlemen, I am a Christian. Six months ago I joined a Baptist church in Nova Scotia, taking vows of loyalty to Jesus Christ. These vows include total abstinence from the use of liquor. I intend to keep those vows, men. I'll be excused now."

With that I left them. For three days I was there. I never saw the bottle again. I was not asked again to drink. I was treated with courtesy and respect—as a Christian nearly always will be when he quietly, courteously, but firmly takes his stand.

Such a story, followed by the hymn "Yield Not to Temptation," or "Go to Dark Gethsemane," will move young people to a sense of dependence on Christ and to new resolve to "dare to be a Daniel."

There are in my files copies of epitaphs from the tombs of great men, inscriptions on public buildings, pamphlets about interesting places and people seen in my travels, and innumerable other items which are usable on occasion in leading people to meaningful worship experiences.

BIOGRAPHY

Biographical material about men living and deceased is rich in facts, quotations, and stories for effective use in planning worship services.

Sermons carry much biographical material. Books abound in this field. Missionary letters and journals are rich in it. Television makes considerable use of biography. Magazines and newspapers carry such data constantly. An alert reader or listener, with a small notebook always within reach, will find such a file thickening with rich resource material.

There follow several quotations and brief stories from biography. They are here to use, but also to illustrate the type of worship material which abounds in the biographies of great missionaries, preachers, statesmen, scientists, military leaders, and great Christians of many walks in life.

1. Francis Asbury, the first Methodist bishop in America, tramped and rode the rude trails and cheerless swamps of the Holston Hills, pouring out his genius on rude "hillbillies." Asked why he spent his life in this seemingly unrewarding way, the stern old warrior replied, "In this labour, we have to encounter hunger, heat, and many restless nights with mosquitoes,

unwholesome provisions, and bad water; were it for silver, I would require a great sum; for the Saviour I ask no reward save that of knowing that I walk in His footsteps."

For a service on sacrifice, consecration, or missions this would be a telling item to use. After brief silence at the close of the account, a solo voice could help greatly by singing "Take Up Thy Cross, the Saviour Said," or "O Master, Let Me Walk with Thee."

2. When Woodrow Wilson, then President of the United States, was in the midst of his historic effort at Geneva, following World War I, to set up the League of Nations as a means toward enduring world peace, he cabled his home for a copy from his files of an epitaph appearing on a tombstone in St. Michael's churchyard, Charleston. The epitaph read thus:

> He withstood his people for his country,
> But his people did homage to the man
> Who held his conscience higher than their praise—
> And his country heaped her honors on the grave of the patriot
> To whom, living, his own righteous self-regard supplied
> Alike the motive and reward.

Such a biographical item could well be used in a service on peace, patriotism, loyalty to conscience, or moral courage. A solo, or responsive reading, using "Dare to Be a Daniel," or "I Would Be True," would be appropriate and moving.

3. One thinks also of the dauntless spirit and speech of William Knibb, pioneer British Baptist missionary to Jamaica, and one of the earliest champions for the emancipation of the slaves. In 1834, long before Lincoln's heroic struggle, and long before the British Parliament's Act of Emancipation, Knibb stood one day before the annual meeting of the Baptist Missionary Society (B.M.S.) and said with deep fervor: "I plead

on behalf of the widows and orphans of those whose innocent blood has been shed. I plead by the blood-streaming back of Catherine Williams, who preferred a dungeon to the surrender of her honour."

Someone pulled his coattail, hoping to stop him. But Knibb went on, unheeding: "I will speak. At the risk of my connection with this Society and all that I hold dear, I stand forward now as the unflinching advocate of immediate emancipation. British Christians must either join with me in an attempt to break the chain with which the African is bound, or leave the work of mercy and the triumphs of the Redeemer unfinished."

And when Knibb sat down after this electrifying message, the chairman, a Dr. Campbell, said with true insight: "This meeting marks the commencement of a new era in the moral history of the world."

Scripture, song, message, pantomime, pictures, used carefully with biographical material such as the above, will produce impressive results in deepening faith, quickening devotion, strengthening high resolution and commitment. Most of all, such material should lead to greater humility and faith in the presence of Him who "worketh in us both to will and to do of his good pleasure" (Phil. 2:13).

QUOTATIONS

Quotations from statements by outstanding men and women of past and present often can be worked helpfully into a worship talk, or related to a Scripture reading, hymn or solo, and the like.

Quotations are without number, of course. Indeed, there are many fine volumes of great thoughts and quotations which are actually series of quotes from eminent men and women of every walk in life. *The New Dictionary of Thoughts,* published by the Doubleday Publishing Company, is familiar to many.

Bartlett's *Familiar Quotations,* published by Little, Brown, and Company, is well known and much used. Walter Fogg's *1000 Sayings of History,* published by Grosset and Dunlap, is worthy of mention. However, the quotations which appeal strongly to us as we read, listen to sermons, hear addresses, are likely to be the ones we can use to best effect and with deepest personal satisfaction. A few of the sort that can be used are listed herewith.

1. Professor Albert Einstein, writing about the Nazi revolution in Germany under Hitler, said:

Being a lover of freedom, when the revolution came in Germany, I looked to the universities to defend it, knowing that they had always boasted of their devotion to the cause of truth; but, no, the universities immediately were silenced. Then I looked to the great editors of the newspapers whose flaming editorials in days gone by had proclaimed their love of freedom; but they, like the universities, were silenced in a few short weeks. Then I looked to the individual writers, who, as literary guides of Germany, had written much and often concerning the place of freedom in modern life; but they, too, were mute. Only the Church stood squarely across the path of Hitler's campaign for suppressing truth. I never had any special interest in the Church before, but now I feel a great affection and admiration because the Church, alone, has had the courage and persistence to stand for intellectual truth and moral freedom.

2. In a public address in Transvaal, South Africa, in 1943, the great statesman and army general, Jan Christian Smuts, said:

Fundamentally the world has no need of a new order or a new plan, but only of the honest and courageous application of the historic Christian idea. Our Christian civilization is based on an eternal order and endless plan in the gospel of Christ. Many new messengers and messages will appear in these times of tribulation. Let us hold on to the light which once shone before us, the greatest light that has ever arisen on the human horizon and can alone lead us to that better world for which we are longing.

Such a quotation in a service entitled "The Light of the World" would be very helpful. A solo of the hymn by that title would be a climax indeed. A group of young people—or older folk, for that matter—might recite one verse each from several passages in which Jesus refers to himself, or is referred to, as the Light of the world.

3. Illustrative of the myriad quotations which can be gathered from missionary sources is this from the life of William Carey, the first Protestant missionary ever to go to the Orient from Britain. Opposed mercilessly in his mission hopes by older Baptist leaders in England, Carey on one occasion burst out: "You excel me in wisdom, especially in seeing difficulties; therefore I will advise with you, but I will effect my task without you. Your caution deadens me if I would permit it."

There is a gallant quotation for use in a service on missions, courage, spiritual independence, or conviction.

4. J. Edgar Hoover, noted American criminologist, can well be quoted for the following testimonial:

I know from my own experience that a deep and sincere belief in God carries the individual through times of great crisis. Our faith can and will result in victory if our belief embraces a consciousness of responsibilities which we must discharge fully if we expect Divine guidance and assistance.

Brief quotations such as this cut across our classifications, of course, and may come from literature, the newspaper, biography, travel, and many other sources. We list these few in this separate category for reasons of emphasis.

5. A moving quotation from Ruskin's *Seven Lamps of Architecture* is valuable for use in connection with church anniver-

saries, cornerstone-laying, Laymen's Sunday, and like occasions. Let us read this fine quotation carefully:

Therefore, when we build, let us think that we build for ever. Let it not be for present delight, nor for present use alone; but let it be such work as our descendants will thank us for, and let us think, as we lay stone on stone, that a time is to come when those stones will be held sacred because our hands have touched them, and that men will say as they look upon the labor and wrought substance of them, "See! this our fathers did for us."

The hymn "We Would Be Building," sung to *Finlandia*, would follow this with great effect. It could be preceded also by a reading from Nehemiah or Ezra concerning the rebuilding of the broken walls of Jerusalem.

6. A call to greater faith and a resultant courage are found in this quotation, in which Martin Luther reproaches Philipp Melanchthon: "From the bottom of my heart I am against these worrying cares which are taking the heart out of you. Why make God a liar in not believing his wonderful promises?"

The hymn "Trust and Obey" would have particular point after such a quotation.

Such quotations abound in biographical books. Book stores will be able to recommend books of biography and others which could be added to a resource library.

It is a useful practice to note on the inside back cover of a book any items which might be used in the future, writing in brackets after each the theme which the item might serve for worship services, or in an address. For example, put in brackets such themes as: missions, conversion, church, conviction, sacrifice, courage, evangelism, faith. This makes it possible to tell almost at a glance whether a given book contains quotations, poems, illustration suitable for use in worship services or in addresses to be prepared. The author puts such back-cover references in three sections: one marked "Q" (for quotable); one marked "P" (for poem); another marked "E.G." (for story or illustration). This, together with the topic in brackets following each item, makes it easy to find material which has struck the person as valuable.

Boxes or file folders would make possible a systematic filing away of worship materials—from magazines, books, story papers, Sunday school lesson books, newspapers—and all the varied materials which come to hand in these days. Also, a good habit to cultivate is that of writing down any illustration or comment which comes to your ear in your conversations and in listening to sermons and addresses. Some of the most effective short illustrations we can use are those which come to us in the adventure of daily life itself. Such treasures are quickly lost and forgotten unless some record is made of them and the record stored away for future use.

If I were adding a word of wisdom to the book of Proverbs I would say, "Words of wisdom gathered in one's leisure will prove a treasure in times of haste."

8

Ten Worship Services for Use

THE FOLLOWING services incorporate many of the ideas presented in preceding chapters. The services should be equally valuable for all age groups above fourteen years. They are designed to produce the attitudes and responses befitting the true worship of God, namely, adoration, confession, thanksgiving, supplication, dedication.

Optional hymns are suggested in some cases, because a single selection might not be known to the worship group or possibly not be included in the hymnbook used. Worship leaders should feel free to make substitutions for suggestions made here. For example, where a prayer poem or prayer hymn is suggested, the leader may prefer to have several sentence prayers or a prayer offered by himself or another person. The materials suggested in these worship services are appropriate and effective when used with care and reverence, but may be replaced by other material suitable to the theme at the discretion of the leader.

It might be mentioned that these ten services of worship may be repeated at later dates with the substitution of new materials selected by leaders, but with the same order and balance of material.

THE SCRIPTURES

CALL TO WORSHIP: "Blessed are the undefiled in the way, who walk in the law of the Lord. Blessed are they that keep his testimonies, and that seek him with their whole heart. . . . Blessed art thou, O Lord: teach me thy statutes."

OPENING PRAYER (*Solo voice sings softly one or two stanzas*): "Spirit of God, Descend upon My Heart."

SCRIPTURE READING:

> *Leader:* The Bible is our worship theme tonight. As we hear it read let us remember the words of the apostle John, in chapter 20 of his Gospel, as he declares the purpose for which the Gospels were written: "These are written, that ye might believe that Jesus is the Christ, the Son of God; and that believing ye might have life through his name."

Responsive Reading: Psalm 119:1–16

PRAYER: There are many moving and exalted prayers in the Scriptures. Let us all unite our hearts and minds in prayer as we hear the prayer of Daniel as recorded in Daniel 9:9–10, 15–19. (*One person may read this prayer fervently as the group bows in reverent silence.*)

HYMN: "Break Thou the Bread of Life"

SCRIPTURE PRESENTATION: The fall of Jerusalem and the second deportation of the Jews took place in the year 586 B.C. There went to Babylon with the exiles some religious leaders, including scribes. By the "waters of Babylon" there was much sorrow, but there was also much danger— danger that the idolatry about them would lead the captives to forget the "faith of their fathers." With no Temple and no synagogues, there remained but one effective way of buttressing the faith of the exiles, and that was through the reading and explaining of the Scriptures, many of which had been taken by the scribes to Babylonia. So the Exile, with all its tragedy, resulted in the copying and recopying of the sacred scrolls and the instruction of the people in their promises and commandments.

In the year 536 B.C. the exiles began to return to Jerusalem. Almost a century later, in 444 B.C., Nehemiah, distressed by news of the desolation of the holy city of Jerusalem as related by a returning relative named Hanani, secured permission of the king, Artaxerxes, to lead an expedition to Jerusalem to direct the rebuilding of the ruined walls and Temple of the city.

Let us hear the gratitude of Ezra, the scribe, who had returned to Jerusalem fourteen years before Nehemiah, as expressed in the book of Ezra, chapter 7, verses 27–28. (*A selected person reads these two verses.*)

Let us hear of the gallant struggle involved in the rebuilding of the city wall. (*Selected persons read: Neh. 3:1–6; 4:1–6; 6:15–16.*)

(*A dramatic scene follows the above introduction. The drama can be simply enacted as follows*):

VOICE (*unseen reader*): Nehemiah 8:1–3. (*As the person reads, EZRA, dressed in flowing Eastern garb, strides to the platform with a large scroll in his hands. Reaching the center of the platform, he signals with upraised hands for all to rise.*)

EZRA (*reading from the scroll*): Deuteronomy 6:4–12; 8:1–11

VOICE: Nehemiah 8:6

PRAYER: Let us bow together in prayer as our thoughts are directed in penitence and desire to the throne of grace by the Ten Commandments, taken one by one:

"I am the Lord thy God. . . . Thou shalt have no other gods before me."

Let us pray for singlehearted devotion to God.

"Thou shalt not make unto thee any graven image."

Let us pray for deliverance from any form of idol-worship.

94

"Thou shalt not take the name of the Lord thy God in vain."

Let us pray for reverence and godly fear before God's holiness.

"Remember the sabbath day, to keep it holy."

Let us pray for grace to give God's day its proper place in our lives.

"Honour thy father and thy mother."

Let us pray that our parents shall have cause to rejoice in us.

"Thou shalt not kill."

Let us pray for respect for the worth of all life—in the factory, on the highways, in all nations; and let us pray that war shall be no more to the ends of the earth.

"Thou shalt not commit adultery."

Let us pray that marriage may be held in ever greater honor in our land.

"Thou shalt not steal."

Let us pray for honesty by employers and employees, and for respect for the rights and needs of others on the part of us all.

"Thou shalt not bear false witness."

Let us pray for charity and generosity of judgment concerning others, remembering the Scripture, "With what judgment ye judge, ye shall be judged."

"Thou shalt not covet."

Let us pray for grace to rejoice in the good fortune of others, and to be thankful for the goodness of God as measured out to us according to his unerring knowledge of our deepest needs unto everlasting life.

(After a brief silence, the leader concludes this period of

prayer by saying, "Hear our prayer, O Lord, as we have approached thee through these hallowed words which thou hast given us. Amen.")

HYMN: "Wonderful Words of Life," or "Standing on the Promises"

OFFERING (*preceded by reading of Col. 3:17 and Rom. 8:32*)

THE MIZPAH BENEDICTION: Genesis 31:49

THE CHURCH

CALL TO WORSHIP: "Ho, every one that thirsteth, come ye to the waters, and he that hath no money; come ye, buy, and eat; yea, come, buy wine and milk without money and without price . . . Incline your ear, and come unto me: hear, and your soul shall live; and I will make an everlasting covenant with you, even the sure mercies of David."

READER: This is God's house. We come here as his guests, at his invitation, and as recipients of his gracious bounty. As we meet here, let us be thankful for those who have gone before us who have made so many places of worship beautiful in design and strong in construction. Being glad for the fine devotion and consecrated workmanship of others, may we, too, resolve to build well the temple of God— that which groweth up in our hearts and that which rises visibly in our land to be seen of men—and to speak to them of the reality of God the Father, Son, and Holy Spirit to those who worship in the churches and who work for the greater glory of him to whom they have been dedicated.

HYMN: "Glorious Things of Thee Are Spoken," or "The Church's One Foundation"

SCRIPTURE AND PRAYER (*Three readers read in turn, and as each finishes, the leader offers the brief sentence prayers printed here.*)

First Reader: Matthew 16:13–19

Prayer: Help each of us, Lord, to know thee in all thy heavenly glory, and to confess our faith and love in word and deed each day.

Second Reader: Ephesians 1:17–23

Prayer: We thank thee, Lord, for the church which thou hast bought with thine own precious blood; help us to make her stronger by the consecration and effectiveness of our services given in her behalf.

Third Reader: Ephesians 3:20–21

Prayer: Let us pray that more and more of the glory of Christ may be seen in his Church and in the lives of all of us.

Solo or Duet: "How Lovely Are Thy Dwellings," or "City of God, How Broad and Far"

First Reader: At the historic Oxford Conference on the life and work of the church, held in 1937, this great statement was written:

"The Church, confessing its faith in redemption through Jesus Christ, sees in every man a brother for whom Christ died. In time of war as in time of peace it should pray not only for the nation in which God has placed it, but also for the enemies of that nation. The Church should witness in word, in sacramental life, and in action, to the reality of the Kingdom of God which transcends the world of nations."

Second Reader: Dr. John A Mackay, well-known American Presybterian leader, writes of the church thus: "The Church . . . lives in the faith that the things for which she stands are the only things that have a future, that history and the Gospel, the human heart and the Cross of Christ, were made for each other. This faith is grounded upon God's revelation that what He wills is fellowship in Jesus Christ." (In *A Preface to Christian Theology*)

OFFERING: A few years ago there was intense feeling in New York City over the proposal to tear down the historic Marble Church of St. Nicholas on Fifth Avenue to make room for just another skyscraper. Among those who argued eloquently that the old church should be spared was an American poet. He wrote this bit of verse:

> Man is a spirit, and symbols are his meat,
> So pull not down the steeple in your monied street—
> Money chimes feebly, matter cannot sing—
> Man is a spirit; let the bells ring.

As we present our offering, let us realize that the church was ordained of Jesus Christ, and has brought more blessing to mankind than any institution known. Let us give now with gratitude for all that the church has meant and for all that Christ hopes to do through its ministry.

LITANY:

Leader: Second century candidates for church membership —"catechumens," as they were known—underwent a period of training and self-discipline. At the climax of the ceremony in which they became members of the church, they declared their commitment in these words, "We enlist with thee, O Christ." Let us make this our group response at the end of each petition in our litany of prayers. Let us pray.

That reconciliation, redemptive love, and sacrificial service may be our task, pursued more vigorously than any war was ever fought,

Group (as leader looks up): We enlist with thee, O Christ.

Leader: That we may purge our lives of every obstruction to the free flow of thy love and forgiveness, and that we may become open channels for thy love and power into the lives of others,

Group: We enlist with thee, O Christ.

Leader: That our homes and all our family life and relationships may fully embody thy purposes and may form effective units in the kingdom of thy righteousness,

Group: We enlist with thee, O Christ.

Leader: That thy love and power, through us thy people, may flow into the life of our communities, cleansing their sordidness and vice, purging their corruption and injustices, binding up the wounds of class hatred and race discrimination, giving them beauty for ugliness and abundance for poverty, making our communities the very frontiers of the kingdom of God,

Group: We enlist with thee, O Christ.

Leader: Hear us, O Lord Jesus Christ, who for us and for our salvation didst face death unafraid, and dost live and reign forever. Amen.

HYMN: "O Zion, Haste," or "I Love Thy Kingdom, Lord"

THE LORD'S PRAYER

MISSIONS

CALL TO WORSHIP:

Leader: "I was glad when they said unto me, Let us go into the house of the Lord."

Group: "O come, let us sing unto the Lord: let us make a joyful noise unto the rock of our salvation."

Leader: "Rejoice the soul of thy servant: for unto Thee, O Lord, do I lift up my soul."

Group: "I will praise thee, O Lord my God, with all my heart: and I will glorify thy name forevermore."

INVOCATION: Almighty God, unto whom all hearts are open, all desires known, and from whom no secrets are hid, cleanse the thoughts of our hearts by the inspiration of thy Holy Spirit that we may the more perfectly love thee, and more worthily magnify thy holy Name, through Jesus Christ our Lord. Amen.

LEADER: Our first hymn, sung to the lovely tune "Irish Melody" (or "Danny Boy"), was written by Rev. W. Y. Fullerton, for many years a missions secretary of the Baptist Union of Great Britain and Ireland. It was sung with great effect and power at the Golden Jubilee Congress of the Baptist World Alliance at London, England, in July, 1955—and sung more than once, because of its great lifting power. We shall stand while the first stanza is sung as a solo; then we shall unite to sing the rest of this great hymn.

HYMN: I cannot tell why He, Whom angels worship,
    Should set His love upon the sons of men,
  Or why, as Shepherd, He should seek the wanderers,
    To bring them back, they know not how or when.
  But this I know, that He was born of Mary
    When Bethlehem's manger was His only home,
  And that He lived at Nazareth and laboured,
    And so the Saviour, Saviour of the world, is come.

  I cannot tell how silently He suffered,
    As with His peace He graced this place of tears,
  Or how His heart upon the Cross was broken,
    The crown of pain to three and thirty years.
  But this I know, He heals the broken-hearted,
    And stays our sin, and calms our lurking fear,
  And lifts the burden from the heavy laden,
    For yet the Saviour, Saviour of the world, is here.

  I cannot tell how He will win the nations,
    How He will claim His earthly heritage,
  How satisfy the needs and aspirations
    Of East and West, of sinner and of sage.

But this I know, all flesh shall see His glory,
  And He shall reap the harvest He has sown,
And some glad day His sun shall shine in splendour
  When He the Saviour, Saviour of the world, is known.

I cannot tell how all the lands shall worship,
  When, at His bidding, every storm is stilled,
Or who can say how great the jubilation
  When all the hearts of men with love are filled.
But this I know, the skies will thrill with rapture,
  And myriad, myriad human voices sing,
And earth to heaven, and heaven to earth, will answer,
  At last the Saviour, Saviour of the world, is King!

LEADER: Dr. Kenneth Scott Latourette, noted American Baptist scholar and church historian, says: "Those who call themselves Christians, and yet do not wish all others to be Christians, are confessing the insecurity of their faith. A church that is not dreaming in terms of presenting the gospel to all men is admitting that it has no message for any man."

This statement is fully supported by John 3:16, that wonderful verse which C. H. Spurgeon called "The Bible in a nutshell." Let us repeat it together.

SCRIPTURE:
  Unison: Psalm 72:1–11
  Reader: Isaiah 55
SOLO: "Whosoever Will," or "Christ for the World We Sing"
BRIEF MESSAGE: based on Peter's vision, from Acts 10 (*This Bible story may be related, with pantomimic dramatic scenes accompanying it.*)
PRAYER PERIOD:
  Two Readers: Acts 17:26–28; Colossians 3:10–12
  Sentence Prayers: for home and foreign missionaries known to the group. (*Leader closes prayer period by*

using the words of the prayer hymn "Lord, Speak to Me, That I May Speak.")

HYMN: "Jesus Shall Reign Where'er the Sun," or "The Light of the World Is Jesus"

SILENT PRAYER (*concluded by the leader's reciting the words of the Great Commission, Matt. 28:18–20*)

STEWARDSHIP

CALL TO WORSHIP: Let us worship God in spirit and in truth.

SOLO (*softly from back of room*): "Where He Leads Me" (*one stanza*)

OPENING PRAYER: "All that we have is Thine, and we are Thine, and life and death and the vast forever are Thine. Our recognition of Thy bounty and of our dependence on Thee for all things has been much too tardy and reluctant. We confess our sin of self-sufficiency and pride, and pray that, in the days to come, we may be wise and grateful stewards of Thy goodness and grace, so that, in all that we do, and are, and hope to be, we may honor Thy holy name and praise Thee aright. Amen."

HYMN: "Must Jesus Bear the Cross Alone" or "O Jesus, I Have Promised"

SCRIPTURE (*read in unison from Bibles*): Mark 10:17–22

READER: Let us hear an important message about money, written by Dr. J. W. Storer, a past president of the Southern Baptist Convention: "In any consideration of the relation of a Christian and money, it is well to remember that the only safeguard against falling in love with money, and the highly possible ensuing deterioration of character, is the clear apprehension of Christ and His Cross, His purpose for the world—and of money as an instrument of unselfish service."

102

STORY: During World War II, a Canadian Baptist pastor was crossing the Rocky Mountains by train. At a stop in a mountain town he sat in his coach, idly glancing at people on the station platform. Suddenly he noticed three well-dressed, bright-looking young women walking down the platform. One of them wore a tam on the front of which was a brass ornament. The pastor could not, at first, tell what the decoration was. He romanticized a bit by thinking it might be an army or air force insignia, given to her by her young husband or sweetheart as he went off to distant battle. He thought of how she was fighting her part of the war by staying at home, praying and waiting for her lover's return.

By this time the girls had walked close enough to enable the watcher to see what the ornament was. To his disillusionment it was not a military insignia at all, but just a brass teddy bear! It was not a symbol of heroism, but of conformity to the fashion of the day. I say this, realizing that an ornament is an innocent vanity, really.

But there was a lesson in that teddy bear! Every Christian should wear an insignia of battle—the insignia of the cross. He is called to battle, to danger, to sacrifice, to hard-won victory. Yet too often when we see Christians at close-up range, we discover that they do not wear a cross at all, but merely a symbol of conformity to the fashions, demands, and self-centeredness of the passing world. Christ summons us to bear a cross. Let us bear it proudly for him.

HYMN: "Jesus, I My Cross Have Taken"

PRAYER: Let us pray, using the words of Francis of Assisi of the long ago:

"Lord, make me an instrument of thy peace. Where there is hatred, let me sow love; where there is doubt, faith; where

103

there is despair, hope; where there is darkness, light; and where there is sadness, joy. O Divine Master, grant that I may not so much seek to be consoled as to console; to be understood, as to understand; to be loved, as to love; for it is in giving that we receive; it is in pardoning that we are pardoned; and it is in dying that we are born unto eternal life."

SOLO: "I Surrender All"

OFFERING: As we present our offering, let us hear the words of an ancient preacher: "What injustice is there, you ask, 'in diligently preserving my own as long as I do not invade the property of others?' Shameless saying!—MY OWN! What is it? From what sacred place hast thou brought it into the world? Thou who hast received the gifts of God, thinkest thou that thou committest no injustice in keeping for thyself alone what would be the means of life to many? It is the bread of the hungry that thou keepest. It is the clothing of the naked that thou lockest up; the money that thou buriest is the redemption of the wretched."

Remembering that money is a means of blessing to others, and an instrument for fashioning the kingdom of God in the hearts and minds of men, let us present an offering to God, the Giver of every good and perfect gift.

CLOSING PRAYER (*in unison*): "Take My Life, and Let It Be" (*first stanza*)

THE MIZPAH BENEDICTION

THE CHRISTIAN HOME

CALL TO WORSHIP: "Jesus, Thou Joy of Loving Hearts" (*first stanza read by leader, second stanza sung quietly by group*)

INVOCATION: We draw near unto thee, O God, in prayer, remembering the assurances of thy Son, our Saviour,

That none can ask of thee without receiving;

That none can seek thee and not find;

That none can knock and find no opening doors.

Help us in this holy hour to know with glad certainty that thou art, and that thou art the rewarder of them that diligently seek thee. Amen.

HYMN: When the youthful Queen Elizabeth of Britain was crowned in a solemn service in Westminster Abbey, she herself chose the processional hymn. It was the majestic one we are now going to sing, "Praise, My Soul, the King of Heaven."

SCRIPTURE:

Leader: Let us hear the Word of God.

Solo: "I Think When I Read That Sweet Story of Old" (*first stanza*)

Scripture: Mark 10:13–16

Solo: "Yet still to His footstool in prayer I may go" (*third stanza*)

Scripture: Luke 2:41–52

HYMN: It seems almost unbelievable that the hymn we are now to sing was written by Joseph Grigg when he was only ten years old. It makes one feel that Joseph must have had the joy of growing up in a home where Christ was honored and obeyed, and where the children were given every encouragement to express their love and faith toward him. Let us sing this moving hymn, "Behold, a Stranger at the door."

LITANY:

Leader: In our responsive prayer, or litany, we shall be guided in our approach to the throne of grace by the Beatitudes of Jesus. They describe the kind of persons which God wants us to be, and speak of the qualities of mind and heart which twice-born people shall possess in a measure and strive, without wearying, to

105

possess in increasing measure. Let us pray, then, responding to each Beatitude with the petition, spoken together, "Grant us this grace, we beseech thee, O Lord."

"Blessed are the poor in spirit: for theirs is the kingdom of heaven."

Group: Grant us this grace, we beseech thee, O Lord.

Leader: "Blessed are they that mourn: for they shall be comforted."

Group: Grant us this grace, we beseech thee, O Lord.

Leader: "Blessed are the meek: for they shall inherit the earth."

Group: Grant us this grace, we beseech thee, O Lord.

Leader: "Blessed are they which do hunger and thirst after righteousness: for they shall be filled."

Group: Grant us this grace, we beseech thee, O Lord.

Leader: "Blessed are the merciful: for they shall obtain mercy."

Group: Grant us this grace, we beseech thee, O Lord.

Leader: "Blessed are the pure in heart: for they shall see God."

Group: Grant us this grace, we beseech thee, O Lord.

Leader: "Blessed are the peacemakers: for they shall be called the children of God."

Group: Grant us this grace, we beseech thee, O Lord.

Leader: "Blessed are they which are persecuted for righteousness' sake: for theirs is the kingdom of heaven."

Group: Grant us this grace, we beseech thee, O Lord.

Leader: Our Heavenly Father, from these inward graces of the heart may there flow out from each of us a testimony and an influence which shall help others to know thee, and love thee, and follow thee unto life eternal. Amen.

STORY: When Dr. T. B. McDormand was field secretary for Christian education in Western Canada some years ago, he came one Saturday afternoon to the Baptist parsonage in a wee village of not more than three hundred population. He had scarcely hung up his hat and put down his suitcase on the floor, when the front door of the house was flung open unceremoniously, without a warning knock. A short, stout man burst in, carrying in his arms a bundle of dog-eared papers which turned out to be practically a library of classical music. The pastor's wife was a fine pianist. She seemed to take this strange intrusion in her stride, for as he said loudly, "I want to sing," she sat down quietly at the piano and awaited his instructions. In amazement the visitor heard this unexpected guest sing song after song from the great masters of music. In a strong, well-disciplined tenor voice he really made "the rafters ring." For over an hour he sang his heart out to a spellbound audience of one— and an accompanist!

When he was through, Dr. McDormand was introduced! The singer turned out to be a Jewish grocer of the village, who, in his youth, had been a professional singer in the states of New York and Pennsylvania.

"How long have you lived in this village?" the visiting pastor asked the grocer.

"Nearly eighteen years," was the somewhat sad reply.

"What family have you?"

"My wife and seven children."

"Do you belong to the Baptist church?"

"Why, no—you see, I am a Jew. I attend Baptist services occasionally, of course."

"How far are you from the nearest synagogue?"

"Edmonton, ninety miles away."

"I am amazed that for eighteen years, with the nearest

107

synagogue ninety miles away, you have maintained your Jewish faith for yourself and for all your children, too."

"But you see, sir, every Jewish home is a synagogue, and every Jewish father a priest before his God," replied the grocer with quiet dignity.

It was then that this Baptist minister realized something of the explanation of the amazing loyalty of Jews to their historic faith. You cannot destroy a faith that centers in the life and relationships of the home! When fathers and mothers resolve to make their homes sanctuaries unto God, and their family life a worshiping unit, you have, as a sure result, an abiding loyalty to the faith which the parents, in turn, received in their homes a generation before. Protestant homes should more and more be dedicated in love and loyalty to the worship and service of God in Jesus Christ.

OFFERING:

> O give me Samuel's ear,
> The open ear, O Lord,
> Alive and quick to hear
> Each whisper of Thy word,
> Like him to answer at Thy call,
> And to obey Thee first of all.

The Old Testament story of Samuel, dedicated to the Lord by his devout mother, Hannah, is a beautiful record of Christian stewardship at work in family life. And Samuel's devotion to the Lord and his Temple is an eloquent tribute to his mother's faith and consecration, and a glorious revelation of how God can use the consecration of even a little child for the working out of his purposes.

Let us make our offering now in a spirit of devotion to God and with earnest desire for the extension of his reign in human hearts everywhere.

108

HYMN: "Happy the Home When God Is There," or "Faith of Our Fathers"

SILENT PRAYER (*followed by the Mizpah Benediction*)

WORLD BROTHERHOOD

LEADER: Let us hear the Word of God about Christian brotherhood

FIRST READER (*seated on platform; gives Scripture reference before reading*): Romans 10:9–15

SOLO VOICE: "Whosoever Will" (*one stanza*)

SECOND READER: Colossians 3:9–13

HYMN (*may be sung by a group from back of room*): "In Christ There Is No East or West"

THIRD READER: Luke 16:19–26

LEADER: From this stern parable we learn that a violation of the claims of brotherhood not only separates us from our brother man, but from God our Maker. Let us remember also the searching words of the Epistle of James: "If a brother or sister be naked, and destitute of daily food, And one of you say unto them, Depart in peace, be ye warmed and filled; notwithstanding ye give them not those things which are needful to the body; what doth it profit? Even so faith, if it hath not works, is dead, being alone."

OFFERING: Let us present an offering at this time, and as we do so, let us think upon the well-known words of the American poet, James Russell Lowell:

> Not what we give, but what we share,
> For the gift without the giver is bare;
> Who gives himself with his alms feeds three—
> Himself, his hungering neighbor, and Me.

HYMN: "Where Cross the Crowded Ways of Life," or "O Master, Let Me Walk with Thee"

STORY: At the Golden Jubilee Congress of the Baptist World Alliance, held in London, England in July, 1955, a German Baptist deaconess—of which there are more than six hundred in full-time Christian service in Eva Hertzer's country —used the following little poem with a big message:

> I thought I heard the voice of God,
> And climbed the highest steeple;
> But God declared, Go down again,
> I dwell among the people.

There is truth for us in those simple lines quoted by Miss Hertzer. Remember how three privileged disciples, after witnessing the glory of the transfiguration, wanted to build three tabernacles in the privacy of the mount and spend the whole future in reverent meditation. But Jesus rebuked them, and led them at once down the mountain slope to where a despairing father with an epileptic son awaited the healing hand of the Master. It is in service, not in selfish solitude and isolation, that we follow most truly in the Master's steps.

SOLO: "Evening Prayer" (*group bowed in prayerful meditation*)

PRAYER: "O Thou who hast made of one blood all nations, and art the Father of the whole human family, grant unto us Thine unworthy servants, a larger measure of understanding, humility, patience, and love in our relationships with our fellow men. Deliver us from harsh judgments, uncharitable words, unjust deeds, and enable us by Thy grace to manifest at all times the spirit of Jesus Christ, who went about doing good, and who taught us that love is of God. Amen."

HYMN: "Lord, Speak to Me, That I May Speak," or "We Give Thee but Thine Own"

BENEDICTION:

The Lord bless thee, and keep thee:
The Lord make his face shine upon thee,
And be gracious unto thee:
The Lord lift up his countenance upon thee,
And give thee peace.

NUMBERS 6:24–26

THE NEW YEAR

CALL TO WORSHIP: "O the depth of the riches both of the wisdom and knowledge of God! . . . For of him, and through him, and to him, are all things: to whom be glory for ever."

SILENT PRAYER: "Our times are in thy hands, O Lord. . . . We spend our years as a tale that is told."

Look to this day!
For it is life, the very life of life.
In its brief course lie all the varieties and realities of your existence:
The bliss of growth;
The glory of action;
The splendor of beauty;
For yesterday is already a dream, and tomorrow is only a vision;
But today, well lived, makes every yesterday
A dream of happiness, and every tomorrow a vision of hope.
Look well, therefore, to this day!

from the SANSKRIT

HYMN: "Jesus, Saviour, Pilot Me"
SCRIPTURE MOSAIC (*references given as read*):
    First Reader: Isaiah 40:28–31
    Second Reader: Matthew 6:25–34
    Third Reader: Romans 12:1–2
    Fourth Reader: Revelation 21:1–4
    All (standing and in unison): Psalm 23

111

SOLO: "Living for Jesus," or "I Do Not Ask, O Lord, that Life May Be a Pleasant Road"

OFFERING: Let us present our offerings in the spirit of these words of Frances Ridley Havergal:

> Oh, let me give
> Out of the gifts Thou freely givest;
> Oh, let me live
> With life abundantly because Thou livest;
> Oh, make me shine
> In darkest places, for Thy light is mine;
> Oh, let me be
> A faithful witness for Thy truth and Thee. Amen.

DRAMATIC FEATURE:

(*Backdrop: Large clock face, or a year of calendar monthly sheets spread out. A group of five young people march across platform, each stopping in spotlight to speak.*)

First Speaker: To me the New Year is a fresh chapter in the book of God's loving providence, and I know that he will write with gracious care for me.

Second Speaker: To me the New Year is an arena in which I must meet many adversaries, but where I am assured of victory through faith in Him by whom we overcome the world.

Third Speaker: To me January 1 is as a door, opening upon a world of adventure and discovery—a door through which I may step into larger fields of service for the Master, finding growing joy under the banner of the cross.

Fourth Speaker: To me the New Year is a highway, stretching toward the City of God, and I must follow it with my eye ever upon the shining goal, my heart fixed upon Christ, my hand held firmly in his.

SOLO: "In the Garden," or "Whisper a Prayer in the Morning"

DIRECTED SILENT PRAYER (*one leader, or a number of leaders, offering the guiding sentences*):

Leader: Let us pray for faith for the New Year, for every day and hour of it; for without faith it is impossible to please God, and by faith we overcome the world.

Period of silence

Leader: Let us pray for courage for the New Year, for our foes are many and determined, and the life in Christ is sure to have its struggles.

Period of silence

Leader: Let us pray for patience—even the patience of unanswered prayer—for the ways of God seem sometimes to be past finding out, and we must await the Spirit's interpretation of all that he permits us to see, and bear, and suffer.

Period of silence

Leader: Let us pray, finally, for the spirit of steadfast love at all times—the love that makes us the children of God; the love that glorifies our human clay; the love that enables us, as co-workers with the Master, to "raise the fallen, cheer the faint, heal the sick, and lead the blind."

Period of silence

HYMN: "Faith Is the Victory," or "Trust and Obey," or "Lead Us, O Father, in the Paths of Peace"

THE MIZPAH BENEDICTION (*Or all stand and repeat in unison John 3:16.*)

EASTER

CALL TO WORSHIP:

Leader (*joyously*): The Lord is risen, as he said!
Group: He is risen indeed, hallelujah.

113

PRAYER OF THANKSGIVING: Almighty God, we bless thee. We praise thy great and holy name, for thou with infinite power has raised up thy Son, our Saviour, from the darkness of the tomb to the glory of life eternal at thy right hand. Thou hast made him victorious over sin and death and given him a name which is above every name, that at the name of Jesus every knee shall bow. Thou hast ordained that those who believe in him by faith may also "rise with him to newness of life." Our hearts rejoice greatly in these provisions of thy grace for us, thy children, through adoption in Christ Jesus, the "firstborn of many brethren."

Fill our hearts, we beseech thee, with the joy of Easter morning, and help us to walk in the light of the Saviour's presence all the days of our lives, so that, when the sun of this earthly life shall set for us, we shall see him face to face and behold in all its fulness the glory which, with our mortal eyes, we have seen as through a glass darkly.

Grant, in Thy great mercy, that the power of the risen and glorified Christ may bring redemption to a growing host around the world, so that men shall behold the coming of thy kingdom, and know with joyous certainty that thou shalt reign forever and ever. Visit us with thy great power; uphold us with thy grace; transform us daily into an ever increasing likeness to him who is the joy of all loving hearts.

With thanksgiving, penitence, and hope we pray. Amen.

SOLO (*as group continues in silent prayer*): "Rejoice, the Lord Is King" (*stanza 3, beginning "His kingdom cannot fail"*)

HYMN: "Jesus Christ Is Risen Today"

RESPONSIVE READING (*may be read in unison, all standing*): Isaiah 53

READING: Hear what Dr. John Caird wrote about the risen Lord, whose presence is "never far from any one of us":

The spirit that was in Christ, and that made all his human life resplendent with the glory and the beauty of the eternal light and love, has not passed away . . . He is near us here and now, the light of all our seeing, the ever-present, inexhaustible fountain of spiritual life and strength. If we do not realize his presence, the hindrance is not in him, but in ourselves. The eye of the soul may be darkened to the heavenly light, the ear dulled or deadened by the tumult of earthly passions to the heavenly voice. But he is never far from any one of us . . . even when in our hardness and coldness we know and think not of it, like light rippling round blind eyes, or sweet music seeking entrance into deaf ears; and nothing but our own dulness hinders it from penetrating and suffusing our souls.

SCRIPTURE (*Use on screen two or three kodachrome slides depicting the events of the resurrection*):

> *Reader:* Luke 23:46–49
>
> *Solo:* "O Sacred Head, Now Wounded" (*stanza 3, beginning "What language shall I borrow"*)
>
> *Reader:* Luke 23:50–56
>
> *Solo (softly):* "Alas! And Did My Saviour Bleed?" (*stanzas 1 and 2*)
>
> *Reader:* Luke 24:1–12
>
> *All Sing:* "Crown Him with Many Crowns," or "The Head That Once Was Crowned with Thorns"

READING: Let us hear the personal testimony of Dr. Theodore F. Adams, president of the Baptist World Alliance, concerning the meaning of the risen Christ for him:

He comes to me as a Living Spirit today as well as a historic person who lived 1900 years ago. He gives me assurance that if I accept him as Saviour and Guide and follow him, I shall be saved from sin and wrong and helped to live as God would have me live. He gives me an ideal to live by—a pattern for life, and helps me as I try to live up to that ideal. He assures me of forgiveness when I fail and helps me to try again and do better. His teachings give me guidance and counsel, truth and ideals, in a world of doubt and fear, and in the midst of changing standards and ways of life. He is a living presence in my daily life—there is a spirit and purpose in me that would not be there but for him. He helps me in the choices of life to know right from wrong and to choose the best of the many good things life offers. He gives me courage and hope in the testing hours of life and in the face of the problems of my generation. He gives me the joy of introducing others to him and to the happiness of the Christian life. He calls me to work with him in his Kingdom and makes me dissatisfied with anything in the life about me that is not in accord with his principles and Spirit. He introduces me to a fellowship that transcends all human barriers of race and creed, of space and time. He gives me in his church a place of worship and training, of fellowship and service. He shows me that, with all my shortcomings, I can be of use to him and to the world mission in which he calls his followers to serve. He helps me day by day to live in love and confidence and inner peace. He assures me of life eternal beyond the grave and calls me to live for eternity now.

SOLO: "Since Jesus Came into My Heart"

PRAYER (*several brief prayers by members*)

OFFERING: In gratitude for God's inexpressible gift to us in Jesus Christ—crucified, risen, and coming again—let us present our offering now as an act of worship and as an expression of faith in the lordship of Christ over all of life and all of history. Let us bring an offering unto him in thankfulness.

HYMN: Let us close this service of worship and devotion by singing a hymn which has become almost the official hymn of Baptist World Alliance congresses, wherever they are held—"All Hail the Power of Jesus' Name."

A CHRISTIAN THANKSGIVING

CALL TO WORSHIP:

Leader: "It is a good thing to give thanks unto the Lord, and to sing praises unto thy name, O most High: To

show forth thy loving-kindness in the morning, and
thy faithfulness every night."

All Sing: "Holy, Holy, Holy" (*one stanza*)

SILENT PRAYER (*as the leader reads slowly, pausing after each
question for a few seconds*):

"Look at the generations of old, and see; did ever any
trust in the Lord, and was confounded? or did any
abide in his fear, and was forsaken? or whom did he
ever despise, that called upon him? For the Lord is
full of compassion and mercy, Longsuffering, and very
pitiful, and forgiveth sins, and saveth in time of
affliction."   ECCLESIASTICUS 2:10–11

HYMN: "Praise the Lord! Ye Heavens, Adore Him," or "When
All Thy Mercies, O My God"

RESPONSIVE READING: Psalm 65 (*Ladies and girls read one
verse, men and boys read the next.*)

SOLO: "Absolutely Tender, Absolutely True," or "Creation's
Lord, We Give Thee Thanks"

SCRIPTURE (*Eight or ten persons read in the order numbered the slips handed to them as they entered the meeting,
each bearing a verse of thanksgiving from the Scriptures,
such as: 1 Thess. 5:18; Psalm 116:17; Psalm 100:2; Rev.
7:12; Rev. 11:17.*)

MESSAGE: A committee of three men from a small church in
Ontario, Canada appeared before a Convention committee to apply for a loan to assist them to build a new, and
much-needed, church building. In answer to questions, they
agreed that they had only 140 members, and that the new
church, costing nearly $90,000, was only one-third covered
by pledges to date. One of the Convention committee said,
"These people are attempting the impossible; I never heard
a more ridiculous proposition in my life." To this one of
the visiting committee replied, "Of course we're attempting

the impossible, but God never performs miracles until his people attempt the impossible!"

How very true that is! In this thanksgiving service we can give hearty thanks that we worship and serve a miracle-working God. He can be limited only by our lack of faith. As we give thanks to the God and Father of Jesus Christ our Lord, let us resolve to trust him more fully, to love him more deeply, to serve him more worthily.

PRAYER: Let us give thanks to God in prayer. Following each prayer suggestion we shall pause for silent prayer.

Let us give thanks for God's providing love and care. (*Period of silence*)

Let us give thanks for Christ's redeeming grace and keeping power. (*Silence*)

Let us give thanks for the joy and peace known by all who walk Christ's way. (*Silence*)

Let us give thanks for the church, built on the foundation of the apostles and prophets, Christ being the chief cornerstone. (*Silence*)

Let us give thanks for the Holy Spirit which guides us into all truth. (*Silence*)

SOLO (*sung softly*): "Thank You, Lord, for Saving My Soul"

OFFERING: Let us remember the words of the Lord Jesus, how he said, "It is more blessed to give than to receive."

HYMN: "Unto the Hills Around," or "O Love That Wilt Not Let Me Go"

BENEDICTION: "The grace of the Lord Jesus Christ be with you all."

CHRISTMAS

CALL TO WORSHIP: "Lord, now lettest thou thy servant depart in peace, according to thy word: For mine eyes have seen thy salvation, Which thou hast prepared before the face of all people; to be a light to lighten the Gentiles, and the glory of thy people Israel." (*Nunc Dimittis* from Luke 2:29–32)

HYMN: "Joy to the World! The Lord Is Come"

RESPONSIVE READING: Luke 1:68–79 (*This, the Benedictus, and the Nunc Dimittis used as our call to worship, constitute the great nativity hymns of the gospel record. One section of the seated group might read the odd-numbered verses; the other section, the even-numbered verses.*)

SCRIPTURE MOSAIC:

Leader: Prophetic voices speak to us out of the Old Testament concerning the long-awaited coming of the Messiah, the Anointed One of God, through whom the Lord of Hosts will fulfil his promises to Israel and to all men. Let us hear these voices as we think of the wonder and glory of the coming of Immanuel, "God with us." First, let us hear the princely prophet, Isaiah. (*Figures robed in Eastern manner appear one at a time, as called; or may—and this is recommended—read from behind a thin white curtain, with a strong spotlight casting their shadows on the curtain as they speak.*)

Isaiah: Isaiah 7:10–14 and 9:6–7

Leader: Now let us hear the voice of Micah as he tells us of the "Coming One."

Micah: Micah 5:2–4

Leader: The prophet Daniel adds his voice to the others.

Daniel: Daniel 7:13–14

Leader: Let Isaiah be heard once more.

Isaiah: Chapters 52:7–10 and 60:1–3

Leader: Let us now hear the last of the prophets, John the Baptist—the only one to whom was given the privilege of looking upon the face of God's Anointed One.

119

John: John 1:10–27 (*Since the words are written of John, rather than spoken by him, the leader may read this portion. In the latter case, the word "concerning" might be added before the words "the last" in the introductory sentence; that is, "let us now hear* concerning *the last. . . .").*

Solo (*from behind the curtain, if one is used*): "It Came upon the Midnight Clear" (*fourth stanza*)

Directed Silent Prayer: Let us pray, each in the sanctuary of his or her own heart, offering thanksgiving and petitions before the throne of grace.

Let us give thanks for the unspeakable gift of God's love in the person of his Son, our Saviour, Jesus Christ. (*Pause*)

Let us give thanks for the infinite grace of God, who, while we were yet sinners, loved us, and, in his Son, made perfect provision for our reconciliation and redemption. (*Pause*)

Let us give thanks for shepherd hearts which thrilled to angel choirs, and for kingly minds which discerned the wondrous truth that the Saviour of the world had come. (*Pause*)

Let us pray that we may, in ever enlarging measure, know the joy of the salvation that is in Jesus Christ who came by way of Bethlehem's manger. (*Pause*)

Let us pray that we may, with shepherds of old, hear the angels sing the praises of the Lamb of God which taketh away the sin of the world; and let us pray that, with wise men of old, we may kneel at the stable bed and offer our worship, our obedience, and our gifts to the Holy Babe. (*Pause*)

Let us pray together the prayer of the family of Christ. (*The Lord's Prayer*)

120

HYMN (*with story and pantomime*): "Silent Night."

Tell the simple story of how a Christmas Eve party was held in an Austrian village, attended amongst others by the village schoolmaster, Franz Gruber, and a musician, Joseph Mohr. Moved by the hallowed thoughts which the Christmas season inspires, Gruber, leaving the party for a few minutes, reappeared with a sheet of paper on which he had written with amazing swiftness the words of "Silent Night" (*Stille Nacht* in German). His friend, Joseph Mohr, impressed by the beauty of the words, composed the lovely tune we know so well, and which he appropriately called *Stille Nacht*, after the opening words of the hymn—"Silent Night."

(*If a German person is present, it would be effective to have him or her sing the second stanza of the hymn in German. A simple manger scene may be depicted by some young people in Eastern garb, forming appropriate tableaux as the hymn progresses. Or if an easier plan is desired, have the whole group march by the manger scene, or tableau, as they sing the first one or two stanzas of the hymn, returning to their seats again and remaining standing to sing such balance of the hymn as remains after all have marched past the manger. Lights are low; the manger scene is lighted by indirect lights.*)

STORY: A Sunday school teacher, feeling that Christmas is too often marked by a desire to "get," and too little associated, as it should be, with loving care for others—especially those in actual need—decided to get his boys to take up a project. He got a list of ten families in the city where there was either sickness, poverty, or recent bereavement. He didn't give the names of the families to his boys, but only the numbers of their houses. Together they prepared baskets of food and packages of needed gifts. Then, on

Christmas Eve, they "played Santa Claus" by visiting the ten homes with their arms full of hampers and gifts. In each place they sang one or two carols and then had a short word of prayer, sometimes by the leader, sometimes by two or three of the boys.

The next Sunday at Sunday school the teacher asked the boys how they felt about the experience. Their replies were just what he hoped they would be. "It has been the best Christmas we ever had"; "I never knew before that the greatest joy we can have is bringing joy to others"; "When I saw the happiness on the face of that crippled boy, I knew what a wonderful thing Christmas should be"; "I found that it is really more fun to give than to get."

So the "experiment" ended, and one boys' class learned firsthand what the true spirit of Christmas is.

POEM:

> The Christ of Christmas tells us clearly
> That all who claim to love Him dearly
> Must learn to live
> And learn to give
> In spirit such as His, more nearly.
>
> The Man of Nazareth calls us plainly
> To live for others—not self—mainly;
> To hear His voice,
> Obey, rejoice—
> Who fails in this lives vainly.
>
> THOMAS BRUCE McDORMAND

OFFERING: In the spirit of the verses we have just heard, let us bring our gifts to Him who gave his only begotten Son for the salvation of the world. (*If an offertory prayer is desired before or after the offering is received, the following could be used:*)

122

With grateful hearts we bring our gifts to Thee, O God, for we are reminded anew of Thy great goodness to us. Help us ever to remember that the gift for which Thy Father-heart most fondly yearns is not the gift of silver or gold, but the gift of our own selves, in glad and loving surrender to Thee; through Jesus Christ our Lord. Amen. (*This is a prayer by J. D. Morrison, D.D.*)

HYMN: "We Would See Jesus; lo! His Star Is Shining," or "I love to hear the story, which angel voices tell"

CLOSING SCRIPTURE (*with all standing, joining hands, and in unison*): John 3:16